MIND WAVES

ARLENE TAYLOR

W. EUGENE BREWER

with **MICHELLE NASH**

Copyright © 2003 by   **Arlene Taylor, Ph. D.**

Publisher   **The Concerned Group, Inc.**
Senior Editor   **Pat Benton**
Copy Editor   **Renee Decker**
Project Coordinator   **Rocki Vanatta**
Cover Illustration &
Graphic Design   **Daniel Potter**

The Concerned Group, Inc.
PO Box 1000, Siloam Springs, Arkansas 72761
800.447.4332

ISBN #0-936785-97-7

CONTENTS

DEDICATION

MindWaves is dedicated to the memory of **Ann Woods Bell** who stimulated our interest in the brain and served as a model for practical application of the information in everyday living.

FOREWARD

"If you can read this, thank a teacher," says the bumper sticker. If you read this book, your brain will thank you. Why? Most brains are involved in reading, and many other things, without fulfillment, enjoyment, or even practical gain. We recite the ABCs and other required educational tasks, yet many still lack the ability to cash in—or even crash in—on doing well, living well, or being well.

Before you assume this is just another health book, or just another "brain" book, think again. Within its covers, *MindWaves* offers clear illustrations and factual morsels that could mean the difference between a life well lived and just marking time in this world, and between being well and simply being.

Thousands of electrochemical events occur within your mind every nanosecond. These events, past and present, are a virtual textbook of memories and moments that are keys to unlocking the wonders and power in your mind.

I am a physician who travels the world in search of discoveries that can bring the rewards of healing and health, which begins and ends in your brain. Why have I linked the content of *MindWaves* with health? The World Health Organization's definition of health (which has not been amended since 1948, an indication of its worldwide acceptance) is the universal standard to measure health. It says:

"Health is a state of complete physical, mental and social well-being and not merely the absence of disease or infirmity."

MindWaves is more than a collection of stories about surfing brains or how nature and nurture impact one's brain. It is also a workbook you can use to achieve a state of health most people don't possess. It will help you unlock the passion in your relationships, discover (or recover) the purpose in life that was imprinted upon your DNA at conception, and foster the unadulterated whole brain intelligence of your children, loved ones and co-workers.

We live in an ever-interconnected world of relationships where one person does make a difference. The brain health of one soul can be more infectious than any Mad Cow virus. The inner soul desires, fuels, hopes, and dreams of a state of complete physical, mental, and social well being.

Each of us deserves more out of life and can have more, even the abundant life. It begins by personally connecting your brain to your hopes, or creating a new vision of desires. Living is more than the mundane day in and day out business of life. Seek the facts that are rooted in timeless truths. You will find them in this book.

But you cannot simply give assent to expert data. Active participation is crucial to change, progress, and to peak performance. If you desire more than a humdrum existence, the mind has the capacity for infinite possibilities. What are you willing to do to grasp such a state of health and well being?

The fact that you have opened *MindWaves* suggests that you possess an unquenchable longing to do more than read a book and thank a teacher. You are becoming conscious of the fact that you are a living textbook and must allow your brain to teach you what cannot be found in a book.

If your brain has dent marks from being sideswiped—or even intentionally broad sided by unknowing parents, teachers, spouses, or bosses—*MindWaves* is definitely a prescription for your healing and whole brain health. But this book is for anybody who is curious about living the good life and making good things happen. I have read it and thank Arlene, Gene, and Michelle for writing it.

Donna L Willis, MD, MPH
Medical Contributor, ABC "The View"
Adjunct Faculty Johns Hopkins University School of Medicine

PREFACE
Nothing Succeeds
Like Success

Whether you have little ability or great ability and excel in many things or only a few; whether you have one talent or ten talents is not of the greatest importance. Who you are and what you do with who you are is what counts! — Anonymous

At the beginning of 2000, many people were talking about what they wanted in the twenty-first century. Media surveys showed that the majority of people wanted to be more successful. Of course, not everyone interprets success to mean the same thing. Some want better health, others improved relationships, others enhanced careers, still others increased financial security, while some want to hone their level of spirituality. Nevertheless, the overall theme was then, and is still, *I want to be more successful in life.*

The question now is, *How does someone make this happen?*

What would you do if you knew of a no-fail way to accomplish your success goal? Especially if it didn't require large amounts of money or contracts with elusive gurus! Would you be interested? What if you knew that it would take some time and effort; but how, when, and where would be up to you? Would you still be interested? Bets are your answer would be a resounding *yes*!

The truth is, a way to increase your likelihood of success *does exist*: It involves understanding and paying attention to your own brain. *MindWaves* is designed to help you get to know your own unique brain—that mysterious, complex, and fascinating organ; that most intricately organized and densely populated expanse of biological real estate in the world--and identify the advantages that it alone possesses.

As the authors of the book, *Living With Our Genes: Why They Matter More than you Think,* put it, "Each of us is born into the world as someone; we spend the rest of our lives trying to find out who." This is a personal journey. No one can do it for you, because your brain is more interested in you than in anyone else on the planet. An old proverb states: "You are the only person who can be yourself; no one else has the qualifications for that job." Your brain wants to collaborate with you and is anxious to do so. Use it for success! *Yours!*

ACKNOWLEDGEMENTS

The authors wish to thank the many individuals who have contributed to the authors' knowledge about the emerging science of brain study. A host of others have contributed through their role modeling, personal friendship, and encouragement. In addition, questions from seminar participants and/or suggestions for practical applications have proved invaluable. A specials thanks goes to those who gave generously of their time to review the manuscript for *MindWaves* and offered helpful feedback, most notably: Pat Brewer, David H. Hegarty, Dr. Donna Willis, Dr. Bernice McCarthy, and Dr. Linda Caviness.

INTRODUCTION
User's Guide for
the Brain 101

Some children end up paying an exorbitant price for having the kind of mind they were born with.
— Mel Levine in *A Mind at a Time*

Have you noticed that every new car you've ever purchased—or microwave or telephone or outdoor grill—has come with an owner's manual? (Not that anyone actually reads it or can even find it when something goes wrong!)

The average person probably realizes that the most important *unit* in this incredible housing called the human body is the brain. For most people who want to understand and effectively use their own brain, an owner's manual or a user's guide is needed.

However, when folks go out to find a book on brains, they are usually dazzled—or is it daunted?—with five pound research books filled with charts, facts, figures, designed more for the scientist, instructor, philosopher, physician, or the graduate student planning to write yet another textbook on the brain.

Where are the pictures? The stories? Where's the readability, the chance that you could actually understand and apply the information?

Think of this book as an owner's manual for the brain. It is designed for the inquiring person. It's for the person who has an inkling that learning about one's own brain and following specific principles could reduce symptoms of depression, burn-out, exhaustion, disease, midlife crisis, minor and major health issues, and relationship stressors. It's for someone who wants to slow down the process of aging and maximize the use of one's unique giftedness.

MindWaves is about the person called *you*—which is really the only place to start. It's easier to understand and live with others when you first understand yourself. Remember Socrates? "Know thyself," he preached, millennia ago.

This book is cutting-edge and inspirational, backed up but not bogged down by research. Moreover, it is relevant and simple—unlike that car manual which, if you *could* have found it, probably wasn't readable.

MindWaves is designed to share insights that can enhance personal and professional growth. It includes information about what brain research suggests we can do for personal and professional improvement. The illustrations used are composites of real-life situations. Names and identifying details have been changed to protect confidentiality. A selected Bibliography contains additional reading suggestions and includes books referred to in Chapters 1-7.

This book is not a biological, medical, or psychological text and does not present an in-depth treatment of specific research findings or topics. The information is not intended to take the place of professional counseling, medical, or psychological care. The authors and the publisher disclaim any liability, either direct or indirect, that results from adherence to any advice contained within, or actions taken, or the application of concepts presented herein.

To paraphrase Mel Levine from his book, *A Mind at a Time*, many of us have paid an enormous price for the type of brains that we received at birth — brains that did not match societal expectations for our gender, or whose innate giftedness was undervalued by society. Nevertheless, we can learn to thrive by identifying, honoring, and living our brain's preferences.

CHAPTER ONE
Finding Your Path –
The Journey Begins

I dreamed of a thousand paths. I awoke to find mine and follow it.
—Oriental Proverb

What is it about our brain, this mystery organ in our head that intrigues or bewilders us so? Most of us are quite talkative when it comes to our faces and bodies. We pay attention to and pamper our fingers and feet, hair and toenails. We discuss the gallbladder, liver, and spleen. We compare notes on procedures that poke, prod, analyze, and even excise our hidden parts. But the mere mention of our brain can cause us to backpedal into a zone of caution, of concern, or insecurity and avoidance.

Literary Link…

"If the human brain were so simple that we could understand it, we would be so simple that we couldn't."
—Emerson M. Pugh

The brain: Where is it? Inside its protective covering that we call our skull. What does it do? That's more complicated. This organ, when unimpaired, allows us to remember and reminisce, ponder and meditate, invent and solve, daydream and retrace, plot and scheme, and design, envision, and celebrate.

Brain Bits...

A piece of your brain the size of a grain of sand has...

- one hundred thousand neurons
- two million axons
- one billion synapses

Most people don't know that their brains also manage their energy resources. Hans Selye, the father of stress management, advocated paying attention to one's "energy bank," and making withdrawals judiciously.

Expending vital life energy inefficiently can shorten our potential longevity by a decade or more. Did you pick up the impact of that? If we don't use our brain energy effectively, we could die earlier. That, among other things, is why brain function is worth investigating.

In life we pay for things in some way—we always give something up to get something else. Since our body's basic medium of exchange is energy, the question is, *How am I using my energy?*

Brain Bits...

Estimated number of brain cells (Neurons)

- A fruit fly has 100,000 neurons
- A mouse has five million neurons
- A monkey has 10 billion neurons
- An adult human being has about 100 billion neurons

Marci's Story

Marci works at a job she was educated to do; feature journalism. She has earned recognition for her stories, and a compilation of her best writing is being published in a journalism textbook. However, Marci is drained professionally. While *appearing* focused and energized, in truth, she drags herself to work every day. Privately, Marci admits, "I can't face another homeless family or desperate drop-out. I'd rather cover current events and do fact reporting."

Jacob's Story

The day Jacob Smithey graduated from law school, he handed his diploma to his father. "There," he said. "I'm finally the lawyer *you* wanted me to be. Now I'm leaving to be the mechanic *I've* always wanted to be."

Is something going on with Marci and Jacob other than attitude and personal choice? Definitely. It's called *preference or bent* or *advantage*—something within our brains that wants us to identify who we really are and who we were meant to be.

Our minds are created to honor that innate giftedness and that yearning. Understanding and following your brain's signals can make a difference between burn-out and midlife crisis, between being stuck or moving ahead successfully, or between barely surviving and thriving.

Literary Link...

Choose a job you love and you'll never work a day in your life.
—Confucious

Innate Giftedness

Each person's brain holds the history and mystery of one's preference—your *innate giftedness*. When you discover yours, the knowledge can result in your choosing to give up some of what exhausts you in exchange for lots of what energizes you. That alone has implications for health, relationships, accomplishments, overall success in life, and potential longevity—to name just a few.

The biochemical potential for preference is believed to be present at birth. Perhaps you've heard it said that someone has a bent for leadership, a knack for fixing things, a gift for music, or a preference for detail? Bent, knack, preference, and gift are all synonyms for the greater understanding of innate giftedness.

Edison's Story

Thomas Edison reportedly said, "My mother was the making of me, she understood me; she let me follow my bent." Edison's mother, a schoolteacher far ahead of her times, made learning fun—after removing him from school where his schoolmaster called Edison's inattentiveness a form of retardation. Together she and Thomas did experiments, (they called it exploring) and today most of us sit under light bulbs created by perhaps the most pure inventive genius who ever lived—a grade-school dropout!

No amount of training can produce innate giftedness, although practice can build competencies and hone skills. For example, if you have a bent for working with your hands, and that leads to a job operating machines, of course you can hone your skills. But persons without such a bent will likely never become as easily competent in a specific area as those born with the brain preference.

If allowed to do so, your brain will prompt you to move toward the best path and will give you hints about how best to travel the journey. Often, however, individuals knowingly or unknowingly shut down its signals. How can you keep from doing that?

Meet Your Brain

Thomas Alva Edison believed that the brain was exceedingly important. So important that he said, "The chief function of your body is to carry your brain around." Interesting! Your brain is an amazing organ—a three-pound universe.

By the fourth day after conception, the brain begins to develop, eventually containing billions of neurons that conduct messages at rates of 400 feet per second and hold 1000 times more information than a twenty-volume encyclopedia. All that, in one brain, and it's as unique as our thumbprint.

As part of the electrical-chemical psychosomatic network, the brain (along with the body) constitutes what is commonly called the *mind*. And, as the saying goes, the mind is a wonderful thing to use, a terrible thing to lose!

Brain Bits...

> The estimated number of nerve cells in our brain, about 100 billion neurons, approximately equals the number of stars in the Milky Way. The estimated number of potential synaptic connections exceeds the number of atoms in our universe!

Conscious and Subconscious

Actually, you have two minds: a conscious mind (what you are paying attention to) and a subconscious mind (what you aren't paying attention to consciously). While you are paying attention to one idea or event, many other processes are occurring simultaneously inside your brain and body, but outside your conscious awareness.

For example, while a man is shopping at the hardware store (conscious awareness) he could also be psychologically or emotionally influenced by an event that occurred that morning at home, what happened that day at work, or by anticipated plans for the evening. He might not specifically notice other shoppers, items on sale, announcements over the loud speaker, or store personnel. But, his subconscious mind might. If he stops to talk with a neighbor, his conscious mind would move from shopping to socializing and whatever turns that might take during the conversation. His subconscious mind might then be consumed with something entirely different.

While your conscious mind focuses on the immediate task, your subconscious mind keeps everything else going in the background environment or other realities. Not only that, and perhaps even more importantly, your subconscious mind is likely the source of all psychosomatic illness. Some researchers estimate that more than 80% of illnesses may originate either in the mind or contain a significant mind component. No wonder Peter McWilliams entitled his book *You Can't Afford the Luxury of a Single Negative Thought.*

Bottom line: Your brain impacts your internal world and plays a key role in creating perceptions, beliefs, reactions, responses, and behaviors. It also influences your interaction with the external world around you.

Brain Bits...

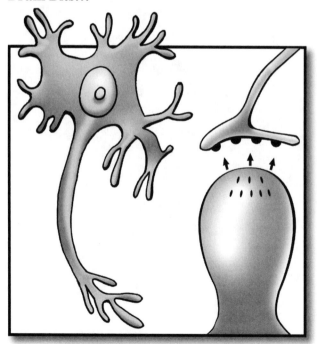

Neuron and Synaptic Gap

More Than One Brain

When speaking about the brain, we are usually referring to all the tissue inside our bony skulls. Most people fail to realize that the brain really consists of several brains or layers, all designed to interconnect and compliment each other. In fact, living life in its fullness requires the ability to integrate the functions of this amazing organ. It can be helpful to describe these layers in terms of groups of functions or systems.

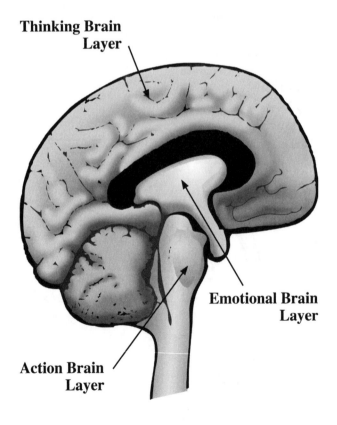

Thinking Brain Layer

Emotional Brain Layer

Action Brain Layer

Cutaway of the Human Brain

A word of caution. We learned more about the brain in the 90's than in all the rest of recorded history; and it's nearly all good! However, what we do not know about how the brain functions still far exceeds what we do know. One needs only to pick up a recent issue of *Time*, *Newsweek*, or *U.S. News & World Report* to realize that new data is being released almost daily. For example, recent researchers, especially Joseph LeDoux, are investigating the origins of human emotions and explains that there may not be one emotional system in the brain, but many. However, for sake of simplicity, we will refer to these layers as the action brain, the emotional brain, and the thinking brain.

Action Brain Layer

This portion of the brain is sometimes referred to as the *sensory/motor* brain, or the *energy* brain. It includes the brain stem, cerebellum, and connections to the spinal cord. It tends to dominate when a threat is perceived. Here we have the fight/flight response capability, activated when safety and survival become top priorities. The action brain also contains the generating plant that provides electricity to power the brain's functions. Overall, the brain runs on approximately the amount of energy required to power a 10 watt light bulb.

Brain Bits...

> The adult human brain weighs about three pounds. It has the consistency of a ripe avocado or partially set jello. One million miles of nerve fibers connect its nerve cells.

Emotional Brain Layer

Sometimes called the *pain-pleasure center,* or *limbic* system, this region is believed to be extremely sensitive to stress. This portion of the brain is also thought to generate emotional impulses and impact relationships, bonding, and memory functions.

Think back to a holiday when you gave someone a gift that he/she did not seem to like. Or recall a time when you received a gift that was absolutely stellar, one that you had wanted for a long time. If your feelings were hurt, or if you felt euphoric, it's more likely that you stored those events in memory and can recall them at will. Emotions are essential for the process of remembering, and this region of the brain contains switching mechanisms to transfer information from short-term to long-term memory.

Do you remember being embarrassed in a classroom or on the job? Have you ever received bad news about a family member? Did someone for whom you cared a great deal ever laugh at you? Do you recall receiving a special honor, award, or prize? Did you win first place in track and field, or the sweepstakes? Have you ever received exceedingly good news about a close friend? If you answered yes to any of these questions, that means, your brain recorded the event. *Any emotional component to an event enhances the likelihood that it will be recorded in long-term memory.* (Whether or not we are able to consciously recall the event is another story!)

In fact, the emotional brain actually translates thinking brain information into a language that can be read by the action brain. If you're walking along and you hear something that causes you to be frightened, the action brain will kick into a protective stress response. When the emotional brain is revved up by trauma, this is associated with a negative or depressed state of mind.

On the other hand, running cool is linked with a positive empowering mindset. If you enter a business establishment, such as a grocery store, for the first time and someone greets you warmly, asking how you are or if you need assistance, your thinking brain sends a signal to your action brain saying, "I feel welcome and comfortable here."

Thinking Brain Layer

The *cerebrum,* or *gray matter,* as it is sometimes called, actually resembles a cap on a toadstool. It is home for conscious thought, although only about 5% of what goes on inside the thinking brain may come to our conscious awareness.

This neo-cortex can anticipate and plan for the future. It can create fantasies, and allow us to imagine and innovate. It can process information at rates of 125 bits of information per second, and human speech at 40 bits per second.

Herein lies the center for your own unique, incredible thinking process preference — your own *innate giftedness.* Specific functions within your thinking brain occur more easily and energy efficiently. That means, simply, that other nonpreferred functions require significantly higher expenditures of energy.

Myths

Our culture has perpetuated some myths that are rapidly losing ground in the light of current brain research. For example: "No pain. No gain."

In fact, the opposite is true. When you are following your brain's advantage and utilizing preferred functions, your brain is just purring along! (Hang on. This is where it gets exciting!) When you use nonpreferred functions, your brain is lugging down. In terms of energy required, the differences may be as great as pennies on the dollar! *Pennies on the dollar*! Physically, the difference in outcome can be plenty of available energy versus discouraging exhaustion.

Every adult should understand his/her brain's preferred functions. Then the trick is simply to use them as much as possible.

Marianne Williamson wrote in her book *A Return to Love*:

> *"We are all meant to shine... And as we let our own light shine, we unconsciously give other people permission to do the same."*

What a concept! That living your own innate giftedness can also free others (encourage them) to do the same. Remember, this is not talking about whether someone is college educated versus on-the-job trained. This simply says that your heart should partner with your brain to figure out the way you function most easily and with the most reward.

The good news is that we will view this process through the lens of only four factors, each of which plays an important role in defining who we are individually:

- Gender Brain Preference
- Extroversion-Introversion Preference
- Sensory Preference
- Thinking Process Preference

And we'll begin with gender brain preference. As Alexander Pope once said, "Tho' all things differ, all agree." Well, that is if we understand!

CHAPTER TWO
Calling Planet Earth...

The struggle of the sexes is the motor of history.
　　　　　　— Alain Robbe-Grillet Djinn

Most of us have heard the myth that men are from Mars and women are from Venus, along with multiple variations on that theme. Truth be told, men are from Earth and women are from Earth and we need to get along with each other here. If either gender were truly from a different planet, he or she could just visit (often!) and then swift back home.

Based on your gender, you will have some built in brain advantages. Many cultures stereotypically reward each gender for thinking and behaving in specific ways. It can be uncomfortable, even difficult, for individuals whose thought patterns and exhibited behaviors differ from these expectations. Again, understanding how your own brain functions most easily is important in the big scheme of things.

Differences Make a Difference
Why do gender brain differences matter? Because if we interact with members of the opposite gender on a regular basis, and most of us do, a communication glitch or misunderstanding based on differences can quickly escalate from a mild skirmish into all out war. Spat or battle, either is a waste of time and energy and can diminish your overall success in life.

Current research shows that neither males nor females know very much about each other's brain uniqueness. As one father said to his little girl as he was reading aloud the story of Adam and Eve: "You know, honey, the problem was not with the apple in the tree as much as with the pair on the ground." Hmmm...

Caution: It is important to avoid ascribing specific characteristics to an entire gender based on the fact that we know one male brain or one female brain very well. Some so-called gender differences may relate more to other factors (e.g., extroversion-introversion preference, sensory system preference, thinking style preference, strong beliefs or expectations) than to gender.

Brain Bits...

> Men's and women's brains are distinctly different. While men have more neurons in the cerebral cortex, the brain's outer layer, women have more neuropil, which contains the processes allowing cell communication. Neuropil is the stuff between axons, and it is fair to say that, traditionally, it has been largely ignored. Most synaptic activity in the brain occurs in neuropil.
> —Gabrielle de Courten-Myers, MD, associate professor of neuropathology at the University of Cincinnati.

Brain Differences

Most of us on this planet are aware of the more obvious gender differences, those that are easily seen. But there are other differences that aren't seen directly, yet often show up in observed behaviors. And yes, these include brain differences between males and females. Dr. Courten-Meyers states that as fact: "Men's and women's brains are distinctly different." Surprised, were you? Probably not!

When we say male and female brains are different, it simply means we acknowledge that they are not alike. It doesn't imply good or bad, desirable or undesirable, and certainly not equal or unequal.

Generalizations

Much of what is now known about the brain and gender differences comes from a variety of research methods including surveys, questionnaires, direct observations, physical measurements, autopsies, blood tests, and brain scans. The results of these research projects are presented as generalizations—conclusions that apply commonly to nearly 70% of the population, with exceptions based on individuality. There are some challenges with generalizations, especially when they are applied to a specific individual.

For example, studies show that, on average, males are larger than females. There are males, however, who are smaller in size than most females and females who are larger than most males. Discovering that one or more generalization doesn't exactly apply to you merely exemplifies your individuality. Avoid discounting the generalization too quickly, however. It may be that you haven't had the opportunity to explore a specific type of function, haven't honed skills for it, or you have a preference that influences the ease with which you approach activities that require use of that specific brain function.

Mara's Story
They were nearly an hour late already. Mara had suggested that Earl stop to check directions, but he hadn't picked up on her suggestion. Finally, she persuaded him to pull into a service station. Hopping out of the car, Mara said to the attendant, "We're lost. Can you help us with directions?"

Earl looked out the car window and heaved a big sigh. He hadn't wanted to stop in the first place. He knew he could find his way there—eventually. Besides, the attendant might not be able to provide directions anyway. Bigger sigh.

Ginni's Story
It was their first cruise on a real ocean-going liner. Almost from the first moment her foot hit the deck, Ginni had no problem finding her way around. Gerry could find his way around, but not nearly as quickly nor as easily as his wife. Wisely, he decided just to let her lead the way and not spend any extra energy trying to figure it out for himself.

Two couples. Two different stories. Both portray challenges with generalizations. This means that almost every sentence in this chapter could begin, "In general the male brain and some female brains..." or "Most female brains and some male brains..." Nevertheless, research generalizations are good places to begin when attempting to better understand gender differences.

Literary Link...

> *The brain is wider than the sky*
> *For put them side by side*
> *The one the other will contain*
> *With ease—and you beside...*
> —Emily Dickinson

Direction Finding and Map Reading

Many male brains are quite adept at finding directions, more so than many female brains. But not all! Do you have a male brain and admit to getting lost more than once, even with a map? Do you have a female brain that reads maps easily and almost never gets lost? You may be in the 30% who don't match the generalization.

For guys who have trouble reading a map, perhaps you have never been given the opportunity to develop that skill. On your next road trip, choose to navigate with the map and leave the driving to someone else!

The skills of map reading and direction finding call on functions housed in the two frontal lobes of the thinking brain. Competencies related to these functions are developed through exploring-type play during childhood, referred to by Gloria Steinem as "field independence".

Field Independence

In early childhood, potential abilities for map reading and direction finding are believed to be present in the brains of both genders. So what happens after about age eight? In our culture, most little girls have their field independence curtailed, probably for safety reasons.

Little boys, on the other hand, get to run around more independently and explore on their own. Boys typically hop on their bikes and take off with the sole purpose of exploring—if their location and environment permits. They may also congregate down at the corner lot and shoot baskets, wrestle, roughhouse, and have less restrictions for all sorts of outdoor activities.

The amount of field independence a child experiences can impact the ease of direction finding and map reading in adulthood. Restricted field independence is associated with a decrease in development of physical opportunities, closely connected to developing visual/spatial skills—later related to direction finding and map reading. This is an excellent example of behaviors in adulthood that may or may not be related to innate ability, and that are related to skill development built through experience.

Spatial exploration (e.g., climbing trees, building forts, riding bikes, moving the body in space —as in sports) is helpful for both boys and girls. Today's kids could still enjoy these activities-parents just might need to be involved with them or be stationed close by.

Asking for Directions - A Whole Different Story

While males are generally better at finding directions and reading maps (this probably won't be a surprise either!), they are less likely to ask for directions. Why? One explanation centers on the difference between male and female brains in terms of hierarchical versus collegial organization.

On a hierarchical organizational chart, whoever has the information is perceived as being higher on the pecking order—closer to the top, so to speak. Therefore, asking for information may be perceived by some male brains as an acknowledgement of being at a lower position, at least metaphorically, and most males don't want to be there.

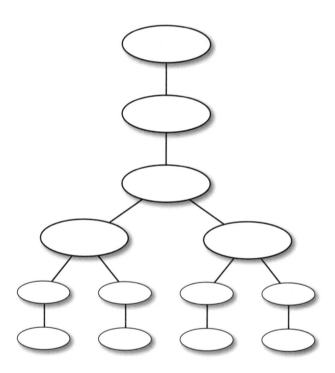

Hierarchical organizational chart

How could you solve this in a cross-gender situation? If you and yours are out looking for the theater and get lost, have the male stop and have the female ask for directions.

In general, the female brain is interested in the quality of the journey or the experience along the way. To the female way of thinking, asking directions in order to arrive before the show begins could enhance the overall experience. Females tend to think of asking directions as a relational event, rather than as a position on a knowledge pecking order.

On a collegial organizational chart, there are fewer levels of pecking order concerns. In fact, many women who found themselves lost would never think of not asking directions. After all, asking questions (to their way of thinking) is often the fastest and most efficient way to obtain information.

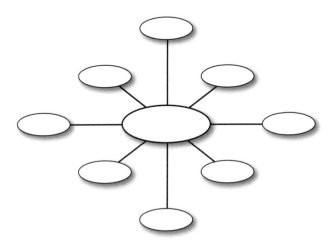

Collegial organizational chart

Nature/Nurture Puzzle

Who we are as individual members of the human race is determined in large part by the nature/nurture puzzle. In this context, the word nature refers to internal genetic programs that tell the brain how to develop and function in relation to genes, chromosomes, and innate preferences.

The word nurture, on the other hand, refers to external environmental factors that act upon the brain to shape its development. This includes exposure to hormones and other substances or activities during gestation, as well as all the external environmental experiences that occur after birth.

Based on the impact of nature/nurture in our own development, plus a host of other factors, each one of us holds a relative position on what we'll refer to as the gender continuum. The stereotypical male brain would be at one end of the gender continuum, the quintessential female brain at the other.

Gender Brain Continuum

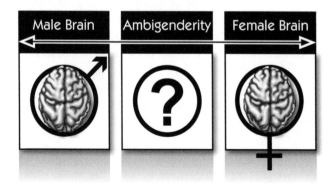

The center position on the continuum represents a band of uncertainty or combination. This range of ambigenderity includes individuals who exhibit external characteristics of both genders, those who have some gender-brain confusion, some who may have chromosomal abnormalities, and still others wherein a male brain resides in a female body and vice versa. Typically, one's brain and body match. That is, a male brain is housed in a male body, and a female brain in a female body.

Corpus Callosum Bridge

Studies show differences in the Corpus Callosum between the brains of males and females, but controversy exists about magnitude. What appears to be consistent is that there's a difference.

Typically in the male brain, the Corpus Callosum—the bridge between the two hemispheres of the thinking brain—consists of relatively fewer connecting fibers of a smaller diameter. This probably results both from its gestational chemical bath and from a later onset of puberty. (A later onset of puberty allows more time for the natural pruning process to occur in the Corpus Callosum.) This means that the male brain is better designed for what is called lateralized or specialized processing, while one part of the male brain is working, the other parts can be idling, so to speak. Consequently, the male brain generally requires less energy second for second.

Lateralization also means that the male brain can do two different cognitive tasks at the same time, as long as each task utilizes functions from a separate cerebral hemisphere.

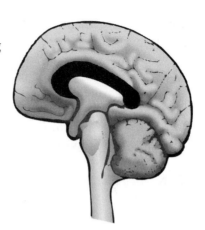

Cutaway showing a **larger** Corpus Callosum in the female brain

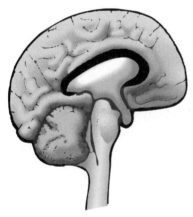

Cutaway showing a **smaller** Callosum Corpus in the male brain

Pete's Story

Pete is putting together a swing set in his backyard and discussing plans with his wife for a surprise birthday party for their daughter. However, if Pete tried to assemble the swing set while creating architectural plans for the garage addition he hoped to begin soon, it might be a different story since both of those tasks utilize functions from the same hemisphere. In this case, he could alternate his attention between working on the swing set and visualizing garage plans. (Or, his wife could finish the swing set while he went to work drawing the plans!).

Generalized versus Lateralized
The female brain has a thicker Corpus Callosum because it did not receive the same type of chemical bath during gestation, and because of an earlier onset of puberty. This difference contributes to a more generalized style of processing, which means that if any part of the female brain is on, it's all on. Consequently, the female brain tends to consume more energy second for second.

Many women excel at multi-tasking. They can perform multiple tasks by rapidly alternating attention from one task to another. In fact, most women can't even imagine not doing several things at once. The first part of stanza one of Maya Angelou's poem "*Woman Work,* illustrates the multi-tasking that many women exhibit in their daily routine:

> I've got the children to tend
> The clothes to mend
> The floor to mop
> The food to shop
> Then the chicken to fry
> The baby to dry
> I got company to feed
> The garden to weed

I've got the shirts to press
The tots to dress...

Tired yet?

Distractions and the Brain
Studies show that the male brain often concentrates better when there is some distraction in the environment. The opposite is true for the female brain. In a quiet environment, females tend to score higher on IQ tests—perhaps due to their more generalized style of brain function and because they often have an increased sensitivity to sounds.

Males, on the other hand, tend to achieve higher IQ scores when there is some noise in the room. Their more lateralized style of brain function helps them to zero in on the task at hand. It probably doesn't hurt, either, that the male brain is often less sensitive to sounds.

Melissa's Story
The hailstorm struck with sudden vengeance. The car was pelted with chunks of ice ranging in size from green peas to green olives. Melissa shook her head and shivered. The sound of ice against metal was overwhelming. "George," she said to her husband, who had been snoozing in the passenger seat, "Are you rested enough to drive? I can't concentrate with all this noise!"

George was and could. They made the change under the next overpass. As the car pulled smoothly onto the highway, Melissa realized that the hail's din didn't seem to faze George at all. In fact, he was concentrating on the highway so completely that at one point it took Melissa three tries to get his attention.

With her more generalized style, Melissa had difficulty blocking out the environmental stimuli and concentrating on driving. George's more lateralized style found it easier to ignore extraneous stimuli and focus on the task at hand—keeping the car on the road!

Advantage of Generalized Style
While Melissa had trouble blocking out the environmental noise due to her generalized brain, there are some advantages. For example, generalized brains tend to react more quickly to an unexpected situation involving both physical and mental stimuli. If a female sees a small child fall out of a tree, she may dash to the scene before she consciously realizes what's happening.

Typically the female brain excels at tasks that involve the rapid perception of details and frequent shifts of attention. And, despite myths, females have 14% fewer accidents per miles driven than men. Generalized reasoning also enables the female brain to have an edge at long-range planning. (Yes, sometimes they are a bit slow getting off the dime and getting the project started.)

Advantage of Lateralized Style
In general, the male brain exhibits a shorter reaction time to a single expected stimulus. This may reflect the goal-oriented, single-mindedness that can occur with a brain that has a more lateralized orientation.

Barry's Story

Barry pulled his new truck up to the crosswalk line in front of the signal light. To his left, engine revving, sat his cousin Margie in her new red Porsche. Barry tooted his horn and gestured toward the red light. Margie nodded and smiled. The light turned green and Barry's tires pealed across the intersection a full six feet ahead. Barry was delighted that his truck had beaten Margie's Porsche.

Barry tended to have a faster reaction time to the single stimulus—the green light. However, Barry needs to be especially careful to avoid tailgating in traffic. When it comes to unexpected stops, the female brain often has the edge.

The male brain tends to excel at short-range planning. Males might outline a detailed schedule for next weekend, but likely not for Christmas vacation next year. When they decide it's necessary, males can take action immediately. They can stop on a dime and get that finger into that proverbial hole in the dyke! Hmmm...

Remember: Different does not mean inferior. It doesn't mean superior. It just means unlike.

Trunk or Cabinet - Metaphor

Metaphors can not only be fun, they can also help us to better understand differences in brain function. Take the trunk versus the cabinet, for example. Using this metaphor, the female brain can be compared to a trunk, a place where everything is together in one or two sections. When looking for something in a trunk, you will often bump into other items, and can even become distracted from what you were originally looking for.

Tala's Story

One Sunday afternoon, Tala, a college coed was pawing through an old cedar chest looking for her junior high journal. Before she got to the journal, she found her favorite childhood doll (later packed for her dorm room), a scrapbook she had put together in fourth grade, her Strawberry Shortcake doll collection, and something that caused her to shriek with delight involving the word "socks." When asked later about finding the journal, Tala said, "Oh yeah, I forgot..." and headed back up to the attic to finish looking for what she had started out to find two hours earlier! Only a "trunk" could have all that fun.

The typical male brain is more like a cabinet that contains many separate drawers, boxes, and compartments with doors or lids. This is why the male brain tends to compartmentalize, segment, and separate the information it is processing. It can put something away behind a little door or in a little box and let it simply sit there until the brain chooses to think about it again. This can also mean that the male brain finds it easier to work with people that it doesn't like. (It sticks that perception in a little compartment and shuts the lid.)

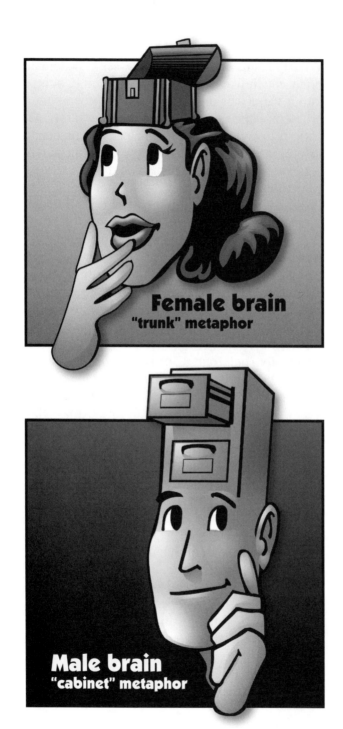

Female brain
"trunk" metaphor

Male brain
"cabinet" metaphor

What happens in these two processes? The female brain, much like digging through a trunk, bumps into a variety of information when processing a problem. This not only may provide additional options to consider, it also can lead to a tendency to integrate, compound, and stew about the newly uncovered information. This could become very confusing to a male brain, whose tendency is to avoid addressing an issue because it has already been "filed" tidily away.

Gender Challenges

Females typically find it more difficult to mentally separate what happens on the job from what happens at home or socially (e.g., the trunk perspective). If the woman's boss criticizes her work, she is more likely to take the criticism personally (not *Your work isn't good*, but rather *You are no good*) and then carry home the painful criticism, transferring it to whatever male figure lives in the house. The female brain may also find it more difficult to work with people that it doesn't like very much—a constant challenge for a generalized brain that keeps bumping into memories or perceptions in that trunk.

With their cabinet perspective, males often find it easier to separate criticism of their behaviors from themselves as individuals (out of sight and out of mind). While this can be a plus, it also can be a negative when there is a need for a man to realize that he, not just his behavior, needs some adjustment in thinking or attitude. This is the challenge for a lateralized brain.

That's why collaboration between the genders can be so effective. Stereotypically, males are more goal oriented, and females more collegial. Two brains, one male and one female (e.g., both vice presidents in the same company) working together should help guarantee that tasks will get done and that morale remains high!

Calculator and Printout Metaphor

Picture the stereotypical male brain as a calculator with printout capability, and the female brain as a calculator without printout capability. Truth is, if you could cut a female brain and a male brain open during thought processing, you would see they are moving through similar processes.

The female, however, who may even arrive at a conclusion more quickly with her generalized style of processing, may find it difficult (if not impossible) to verbalize the sequential steps her brain went through to arrive at the solution because there is no printout capability. In the end, a female might be shamed for a perceived lack in this area, and if pressed, may try to come up with "reasons for the reason."

When problem-solving, the male brain tends to function as a calculator that is wired with a printout capability. Although it may take longer to arrive at a solution, the male brain can usually identify (metaphorically "print out") the sequential steps his brain went through to arrive at an answer. He can articulate these steps, too, if he chooses to do so. Males who fail to understand that all brains do not come equipped with printout capability might discount female answers when a printout of the steps is not forthcoming. Can you imagine how this might be frustrating for males and females?

Using her generalized brain, Mindy suggests a destination when discussing vacation plans. "Why did you suggest that?" Steve asks. Because she finds it difficult to sequentially rehearse the steps her brain went through, her suggestion is somehow discredited in his eyes.

Imagine the implications in a courtroom setting. Questions are being directed to a female witness:

"What gave you the idea that Bob Jones was the thief?" Pause. "I just knew. I had a feeling..."

The female jury members nod, the males shake their heads, and one or two even roll their eyes.

To Shop or Not to Shop

The tendency of the female brain to be more experience—oriented than goal-oriented shows in a variety of ways, and shopping is one of them! One man cleverly described the typical gender shopping experience: "Males hunt, and women browse." Rarely do cross-gender couples refer to each other as their "favorite shopping partners."

The "experience" of browsing and comparative shopping is one of the joys for many women. Even though car shopping can be comparative to men, it still becomes more of a hunt since research and testing is usually involved.

Sally's Story

When Sally invited her husband, Joe, to go to the mall with her, he paused for a moment and then asked, "What's on your list?" (Huge clue regarding brain function here.) Sally, who of course did not have a written list, said, "Uh, I want to look for a peach sweater, try on some shoes, and maybe even have lunch." Joe's second question was: "How long do you expect to be gone?" (Alarms were starting to sound.)

Sally knew that Joe had no plans for that day, so she couldn't understand why it mattered. In the end, Joe went shopping. At the mall he set out at a brisk pace and headed into a women's clothing store. By the time Sally got there he had rummaged through an entire rack, found a peach (well, it was really more orange!) sweater and said, "Here. And it's on sale. We can cross this one off your list."

What happened to comparison shopping? The joy of the experience? The companionship Sally had looked forward to? Joe was giving her the gift of a shopping partner, but the male shopping hunt is a much different design than two women chitchatting, browsing around, enjoying the pleasure of being waited on for lunch, and literally killing an afternoon.

For a guy it's more competitive, like throwing darts—Ready...Aim...Bull's eye!

For a gal, it's more like eating an ice cream cone—the experience of enjoying the treat is what is important, and winning could even mean being the last to finish.

Probably the best that a typical male and a typical female can do when it comes to shopping is to set clear parameters in advance, stick to them, and chuckle about the differences. Or, have him meet her for lunch in the mall. It will save a lot of brain energy for both parties—especially if she's on time! That's not to say a male brain and a female brain can't shop together in equanimity. Once again, it's all about understanding.

Literary Link...

> A trifling matter, and fussy of me, but we all have our little ways.
> —*The House at Pooh Corner,* Milne

Gender Differences and Emotion

Undoubtedly, male or female, you have sensed this all along: Studies show that women tend to recall emotional events better than men do. "The wiring of emotional experience and the coding of that experience into memory is much more tightly integrated in women than in men," says Turhan Carili, assistant professor of psychology at State University of New York, Stony Brook. The folklore that "husbands never remember marital spats and wives never forget..." is now backed up by research. (This study may also shed light on why clinical depression is more common in women.)

Preliminary research suggests that the amygdalae—brain structures that have to do with emotions and memory—grow more quickly in boys than in girls, but males generally don't articulate their deep emotions as frequently or as descriptively as females. Males are much more likely than females to express emotions through actions rather than words.

That's why during a crisis such as the death or illness of a family member or friend, men tend to react by doing something rather than saying something. A woman might comfort a grieving widow by visiting with her in her home or inviting her to lunch; a man might mow her lawn or fix her car. A woman would more likely share sad feelings over an ill child; a man will be on the Internet trying to find cures.

Thinking and Feeling States

Typically, male brains have more difficulty shifting from thinking to feeling states. A classic story from the late 1800s about the differences in gender thinking is "The Revolt of Mother," by Mary E. Wilkins. It begins with Mother (Sarah Penn) confronting Father:

> *"Father!"*

> *"What is it?"*

> *"What are them men diggin' over there in the field for?"*

> *There was a sudden dropping and enlarging of the lower part of the old man's face, as if some heavy weight had settled therein; he shut his mouth tight, and went on harnessing the great bay mare. He hustled the collar on to her neck with a jerk.*

> *"Father!"*

> *The old man slapped the saddle upon the mare's back.*

> *"Look here, father, I want to know what
> them men are diggin' over in the field for,
> an' I'm goin' to know."*

> *"I wish you'd go into the house, mother,
> an' 'tend to your own affairs," the
> old man said then. He ran his words
> together, and his speech was almost as
> inarticulate as a growl.*

> *But the woman understood; it was her
> most native tongue. "I ain't goin' into
> the house till you tell me what them men
> are doin' over there in the field," said she.*

As the story progresses, we learn that Father is building another barn, even though Mother has lived for forty years in a house that was too small, unfinished, shabby, and completely unsuitable for daily living or any sort of entertaining. Their daughter's wedding was coming up and Sarah wanted a brand new house. She put it to Adoniram straight:

> *"You've built sheds an' cow-houses an'
> one new barn, an' now you're goin' to
> build another. Father, I want to know if
> you think it's right. You're lodgin' your
> dumb beasts better than you are your own
> flesh an' blood..."*

But he built the barn anyway.

Just days before the new cows were to move in, Adoniram Penn had to make an emergency trip. During his three-day absence, Sarah Penn and her two children frantically emptied everything from the little old house and triumphantly moved into the big new barn. Then Father came home.

> *"I've made it the subject of prayer, an' it's betwixt me an' the Lord...The house wa'n't fit for us to live in any longer, an' I made up my mind I wa'n't goin' to stay there."*

> *...The old man's shoulders heaved: he was weeping. Adoniram was like a fortress whose walls had no active resistance, and went down the instant the right besieging tools were used.*
> [And the kicker...]
> *"Why, mother,"* he said, hoarsely, *"I hadn't no idée you was so set on't as all this comes to."*

"No idea?" Probably not! All those years Adoniram Penn just plain didn't "get it." His lateralized thinking drove him toward his goals in a one-track direction, tuning out his wife's needs and pleas.

Hope for Relationship Success
It's past time to make more functional decisions about the ways in which we relate to members of both genders.

Myth: "Anything you can do, I can do better..."
Fact: Actually, maybe not. And...so what?

The greatest challenge of all: To your own brain gender be true.

Celebrate joyfully who you are — generalized

or lateralized, trunk or cabinet, printout or no printout capability. Each style is desirable and is part and parcel of who we are. But all brains are certainly not alike.

Does knowing your gender brain preference lock you into functioning in a specific style? No. It can help you to realize why you tend to expend more energy and perhaps be less successful when you try to consistently use your brain in a manner that doesn't match its innate strengths.

Understanding the type of gender brain you have and recognizing similarities and differences of your closest loved ones or work associates can enhance your relationships. Of course, merely knowing the differences doesn't remove them. But it does allow you more options. It can empower you to identify those options and make collaborative choices that honor each other's differences without taking them personally or letting them interfere with achieving positive outcomes. It sets you free to select, by design, a more effective behavior in a specific situation.

Remember: *Different* does not mean inferior. It does not mean superior. It only means *unlike!*

Are you getting that? It took poor old Adoniram forty years. Most of us could probably do better—if we want to!

A final note on gender brain preference
Dame Ivy Compton-Burnett (1884-1969) said, "There is more difference within the sexes than between them." Societal myths have caused many to be reluctant to investigate their strengths, quite

simply because they do not believe their natural talents fit the expectations. It may not be easy to be female and excel in math or debate. It may be somewhat uncomfortable to be male and excel in connection or nurturing. Deep inside our psyche each of us needs to be viewed as an individual worthy of respect. This need is so powerful many have risked life and limb in order to fulfill it.

In all our interactions, from our playground squabbles, to the establishment of our families, to the corporate boardroom, we must learn to treat people with the respect they deserve as human beings. For increased effectiveness, long-term health and happiness, and to make the contribution that only you can bring to this world, remember the words of Martin Buber:

> "Every person born into this world represents something new, something that never existed before. It is the duty of every person to know that there has never been anyone like her/him in the world, for if there had been, there would be no need to be."

Every single person that is born into this world includes you.

CHAPTER THREE
I'm Okay, What's Your Problem?

*"How glorious it is—and how painful
also—to be an exception."*
                    —Alfred de Musset, 1857

Michael's Story

Mrs. Tanner was certain that he was the quietest student she had ever taught in her twenty-year career. Michael was placed in her room for both seventh and eighth grade English, and appeared to be unusually and painfully shy. While his work was always done and turned in on time, his teacher hardly knew the sound of his voice.

Michael worked alone, spent free time alone, and ate alone. But this is not to say that he appeared unhappy or depressed. He actually had a pleasant face and often smiled, but mostly to himself, looking down.

When Michael completed the eighth grade, Mrs. Tanner wondered what would happen to him in high school where loud and crazy ruled. She rarely saw him after that, and, of course, he wasn't the type of student to return for a visit.

On the other hand, Dolly was as different from Michael as day is from night. The sound of her voice was the first one Mrs. Tanner heard in the morning (often it continued after the opening bell) and was usually the last sound she heard in the afternoon.

Dolly was rarely alone. She was in the middle of whatever was happening in the schoolroom, in the cafeteria, and on the playground. She was noisy and at times, argumentative. It's no surprise that Dolly and Michael rubbed each other the wrong way; like cats and dogs, oil and water, extroverts and introverts.

Literary Link...

> People who make no noise are dangerous.
> —Jean de LaFontaine, *Fable*, 1678
> Noise is the most impertinent of all forms of interruption.
> —Arthur Schopnhauer, Studies in Pessimism, 1851

Extroversion, Ambiversion, and Introversion

Growing up, most of us developed some stereotypical beliefs about the term *introverted*. You may even have described individuals you thought were introverted, using words such as shy, retiring, loner, hard-to-get-to-know, stuck up, or wall flower.

What about the term *extroverted*? Try words such as outgoing, lively, in-the-public-eye, life of the party, overactive, or class clown.

In suggests inward; *ex* suggests outward. And so there are counterparts of attention—one directed within the self (introversion), the other directed outside the self (extroversion, or extraversion as used by Jung and others). And *ambi* suggests parts of both. It forms the basis for *ambiversion*, a word that describes the state of being neither extremely extroverted nor extremely introverted, but expressing aspects of both.

These differing states are sometimes expressed as a continuum. Extreme extroversion at one end, extreme introversion at the other end, and ambiversion in the middle. The continuum might look something like this.

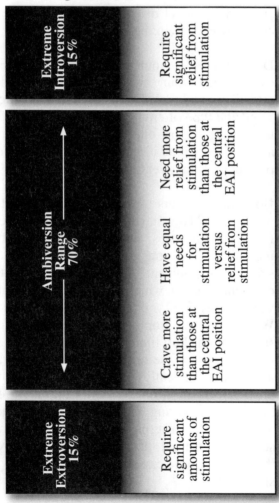

EAI Continuum

Extreme Extroversion 15%	Ambiversion Range 70%			Extreme Introversion 15%
Require significant amounts of stimulation	Crave more stimulation than those at the central EAI position	Have equal needs for stimulation versus relief from stimulation	Need more relief from stimulation than those at the central EAI position	Require significant relief from stimulation

Vital Concepts

Our relative position on the EAI Continuum (e.g., extroversion, ambiversion, or introversion) may be as vital to one's sense of self as thinking process preference (addressed in Chapter Five). Carl Jung, renowned Swiss psychologist and researcher, certainly thought so. Since these terms really apply to *environmental comfort zones*, perhaps a person does need to sustain a comfortable level of stimulation before he/she can fully engage in thinking functions.

Depending on your position on the EAI Continuum, your brain will function most effectively and feel alive, alert, and energetic in a specific type of environment—one that offers lots of stimulation, one that contains a moderate amount of stimulation, or one that provides protection from overstimulation.

How have others described you from this perspective? How have you described yourself? Have you, at times, sensed that you didn't fit in with expectations for stimulation in your specific environment? Can you already identify environments in which you feel comfortable versus those that you try to avoid at all costs? What about environments in which you can survive for a short time but then just *have to get out of there*, or the ones you gravitate toward almost automatically? Figuring out your own preferred position on the EAI Continuum can be like discovering buried gold. It can help you evaluate differing environments from a somewhat neutral position rather than from the position of expectations or shoulds or shouldn'ts.

Three Types of Brains

It can be helpful to think of this concept in terms of three differing types of brains. (It's really not quite that simple—it's more of a range of differing types of brain).

Extroverted Brain

This type of brain has high needs for stimulation and low needs for relief from stimulation. We often refer to this type of brain as being extremely extroverted. Approximately 15% of the population fall into this category. These individuals gravitate toward stimulating environments that may, or may not, involve people. (Some individuals prefer to obtain their stimulation from people, others don't). Those with extremely extroverted brains often perform better (socially, physically, or academically) under pressure or in the face of competition because of the added stimulation these situations provide. In effect, the stimulation serves to *wake up* their brains. Without sufficient amounts of stimulation, they may literally feel sleepy.

Ambiverted Brain

This type of brain has relatively equal needs for stimulation versus relief from stimulation. Approximately 70% of the population fall into this ambiversion range. The brains of these individuals are neither extremely extroverted nor extremely introverted. Sometimes they crave stimulation, and sometimes they need relief from stimulation. Time spent in extremely stimulating environments, however enjoyable, needs to be compensated for with recovery time spent in environments that are much less stimulating.

Introverted Brain

The introverted brain has low needs for stimulation and high needs for relief from stimulation. The brains of these individuals actually need to be protected at times. We usually refer to this type of brain as being extremely introverted. Approximately 15% of the population is believed to fall into this category. When this type of brain becomes overstimulated it tries to shut out further input, but that does not mean it literally shuts down. Rather, introverts retreat almost automatically to block out additional stimuli while they evaluate, process, search for insight, and reflect on what's been going on around them. These individuals may perform less well under the pressure of exams, conflict, or competition because of the high level of stimulation inherent in those situations.

Part of the Package

Just as gender brain preference is in place when we *come out the shoot*, babies are believed to arrive on the scene with their own innate position on the EAI Continuum already assigned. Potentially, the extremes can be identified within days of birth. If you're a parent of an extreme, you might have researched this in your own personal laboratory—your home.

An infant with an extremely extroverted brain may sleep fewer hours, may stop crying only when passed around the room to a dozen different caregivers, and may rattle the crib or bang its head on the bed frame in an effort to obtain stimulation. Some of you might be saying right now, *Yes, I tore my hair out with just such a child. He/she was always getting into some type of mischief!* Obviously, looking for stimulation!

An infant with an extremely introverted brain may sleep longer hours and may stop crying only when placed in a quiet darkened room, or when allowed to lie quietly instead of being rocked. And this child is more likely to become ill when over-stimulated. Parents of this type of child (especially if it was the first child) might have thought, "Piece of cake. Let's have a dozen!" only to discover that the second child's brain was very different in terms of placement on the EAI Continuum. On the other hand, an extremely extroverted parent might have thought something was wrong with the child because it was so different from the parent, and vice versa.

The majority of children fall within the range of ambiversion, having almost equal needs for stimulation and relief from stimulation. Identifying one's position in the ambiversion range occurs by exclusion—that is, if the child is neither extremely extroverted nor extremely introverted, then he/she likely falls in the ambiversion range. A caregiver's job is to figure out what that child's brain craves (stimulation or relief from stimulation) and under what circumstances, and then to help the child understand which environments are optimum, and which ones can be stressful for the brain.

It can get a little worrisome when your two year old goes into the bedroom and shuts the door or hides behind the couch. At the same time it can get very exhausting if your two year old never wants to play alone. And, if not enough is going on (according to its brain), decides to take matters into his/her own hands! Of course, life with toddlers can be exhausting with any brain preference. However, understanding some of these factors can make all the difference in the world in terms of our responses.

Societal Rewards Have Changed

In Europe, during the Middle Ages, introversion was often valued over extroversion. That is, individuals with brains that leaned toward introversion were often rewarded over those whose brains leaned toward extroversion. Those with extremely introverted brains often gravitated to a religious order, and it was considered a high honor to be in this category. Away from the hustle and bustle of materialism, they found solitude and validation for their abilities to study, copy the scriptures or other books, write, compose, or illustrate. Some found that such an environment was conducive to developing a spiritual connection with a Higher Power.

As the shift toward industrialization occurred, extroversion came to be more highly valued. Gradually, it was encouraged and rewarded to the point that introversion actually became devalued. As religious orders became secularized, there were fewer protected environments available to individuals whose brains were extremely introverted.

In any event, our present society doesn't deal effectively with either of the extremes— introversion or extroversion. Extremely extroverted children are often punished and/ or medicated, in an effort to dampen their stimulation-seeking behaviors.

Extremely introverted children are often pushed toward competition and/or punished for a perceived lack of participation. Very shy teenagers may be laughed at, shunned, or excluded since they are too quiet or perhaps too difficult for other students to get to know.

As adults, extremely extroverted males may get by a bit easier than extremely extroverted females who don't meet societal expectations for "nice" women. Neither gender is rewarded for being extremely introverted, although an introverted woman might have an easier time because she might be viewed as more "feminine."

Our American society typically rewards two positions on the EAI Continuum. Both fall in the ambiversion range: the position right in the center and the one leaning toward extroversion.

Camera Metaphor

Imagine that each brain has its own camera with a uniquely sized aperture. If the opening to the brain's camera is relatively small in diameter, that type of brain needs to take lots of pictures to obtain the stimulation it requires. A great deal of stimulation (action and input) is required in this environment. And, if there is insufficient stimulation, these individuals try to create their own. They may even self-medicate with chemical stimulants such as caffeine or other substances. That's the extremely extroverted brain.

If the brain's camera has a large aperture, it can take in huge amounts of data second for second and can become overloaded and over-stimulated quickly. A very active environment can be overwhelming. That describes the extremely introverted brain.

And, 70% of the population has a moderately sized aperture with nearly equal needs for stimulation and relief from stimulation.

Differing Apertures

As stated by Alfred de Musset, along with the discomfort of being an exception, there is also a certain glory. Both the pain and the glory of extreme extroversion and extreme introversion represent a specific type of giftedness and each can thrive in the appropriate environment. For example, extreme extroverts can often function in situations that could almost immobilize an extreme introvert, while extreme introverts can process information internally or in secluded locations in a manner that could put an extreme extrovert to sleep.

Extreme Extroversion

Extreme extroverts are great participators (although not necessarily team players). They are more likely to engage in a good debate or roughhousing. They tend to have good short-term memory, but may also forget things more quickly. If they read, it's often to gain additional stimulation. If there's enough going on in the environment, they may avoid reading in favor of other more active types of participation.

Extreme extroverts tend to score higher on positive current mood scales—which means they might seem happier than introverts, perhaps because they are less introspective. They are more likely to get into trouble in school, especially if the specific classroom is geared for the more introverted brain (which many classrooms are). When these individuals are not getting enough stimulation, they can become quickly bored and may even fall asleep—if they haven't already gotten into trouble during their search for stimulation!

They can excel at activities that would be virtually impossible for extreme introverts: negotiating in situations of high-tension, competing under situations of high-stress, participating on a SWAT team. Their extreme giftedness pulls them through.

In S.E. Hinton's book *The Outsiders*, we are introduced to gang members from both sides of town: the Socs and the Greasers. As Ponyboy narrates the story, he describes his Greaser gang friends. One stands out—Two Bit, the "wisecracker of the bunch." Here is a classic description of an extreme extrovert.

"...He couldn't stop making funny remarks to save his life. You couldn't shut up that guy...Life was one big joke to Two-Bit...He was always smarting off to the cops. He really couldn't help it. Everything he said was so irresistibly funny that he just had to let the police in on it to brighten up their dull lives. (That's the way he explained it to me.) [Regarding school] He just went for kicks..."

Ever go to school or work with someone like that? Was that someone you?

Extreme Introversion

Extreme introverts tend to be the observers in life. You may see them sitting or standing alone. They may go off and take a walk or a nap when things around them get too busy. They may like people very much but they usually prefer to take them in very small groups, or on a one-on-one basis. They often enjoy face-to-face conversations when the subject is of interest to them, but often they would just as soon use e-mail! They tend to do better at the university level where there is more opportunity for independent study. Unfortunately, an extreme introvert can feel like a misfit in our society.

Jared's Story

Jared did feel like a misfit. Not just in society, but in his own home! For as far back as he could remember he'd always been at odds with the other three members of his family. Oh, they loved each other. They really did. But they definately didn't understand each other. They were in a constant tug of war.

It would go like this: "Come on, Jared, let's go have a game of basketball." When Jared invariably replied, "You go ahead, I think I'll stay here and read a book or work on the computer," someone was sure to climb his frame. His parents and younger brother wondered why he didn't want to do things with them, and why he was so often sick, which meant he couldn't participate.

Jared's extremely introverted brain was simply trying to grow up in an environment orchestrated by three extremely extroverted brains. Not even ambiverted brains. Extremely extroverted brains! The poor chap was dying from too much stimulation! No wonder he was sick more frequently than the other family members.

Literary Link...

> The soul selects her own society, then shuts the door to her divine majority. Present no more...Then close the valves of her attention like stone. (Emily Dickinson —often described as a classic introvert, Dickinson kept herself secluded behind closed doors for years until her death. Through her letters and poetry, we see not only an introverted brain, but also a brain wanting to be known, a person anxious to be revealed on her own terms.)

Harold's Story

Upon graduation from high school, Harold got a summer job selling children's home-library books door-to-door. It was a good opportunity to earn a major portion of his college tuition, so he applied himself to the task and worked long hours. Sales were slow, however, and Harold was near exhaustion and burnout. It was difficult for him to face rejection, especially when it was meted out even before he was able to display the wonderful children's books. Many days he couldn't face knocking on the first door. Discouragement was moving toward depression. He simply could not do this any more, college tuition or no college tuition!

Fortunately, Harold found another job as an equipment operator on a highway construction project. The job required twelve-hour days, but the work seemed like play compared to selling books. Several years later, this young man attended a brain-function seminar and discovered that extreme introversion and door-to-door-sales are not very compatible matches, regardless of the person's age, the product's quality, or even one's own desire. How affirming to realize that his lack of success (some of his friends called it an outright failure) as a salesperson wasn't due to lack of purpose, nor to some defect in his character. The activity was too energy-exhaustive for his highly introverted brain.

Can you imagine an extreme extrovert doing computer programming in a cubicle, composing music in a solitary studio, doing research in a one-person lab, or working as a bookkeeper or interior decorator? If not completely stir crazy, or falling asleep on the job, the solitary intensity of this could drive him/her right up the wall and onto the ceiling.

What about an extreme introvert working as a negotiator, running a small retail business and trying to be all things to all customers, selling advertising, practicing as a courtroom attorney in high-profile cases, or trying to succeed as a telemarketer? Imagine how exhausting and painful that could be for an introverted brain.

Mark's Story
Mark was in high demand. The leaders of his denomination considered him to be one of their finest and most inspirational speakers, and his dozen-plus books topped out in sales. For years he had been a traveling evangelist, but when he finally accepted a job as senior pastor for a large

university-affiliated church, the congregation was thrilled. Week after week, Mark delivered inspiring, thought-provoking, and exquisitely crafted homilies.

Each week when the sermon was concluded, however, Mark (like Elvis) would disappear. People wanted to shake his hand and thump his back, but he was out of there! Finally the congregation, choosing to be offended by what they perceived to be Mark's rude social behaviors, approached the church board. "This guy isn't a pastor," they complained, "he hardly even speaks to us!"

It was true. Mark was not a typical pastor. Certainly not the type of pastor that many congregations have come to expect. His was an extremely introverted brain. Being in front of the podium put him in a one-to-one situation with his congregation. Not a problem. Take him out of the podium and put him in the midst of a large group of people, however, and his eyes would glaze over. He would freeze. The congregation needed to decide whether they wanted a fantastic preacher or the quintessential pastor.

The church board finally concluded that there were other individuals on staff who could shake hands at the door, make house visits, and show up at potlucks and picnics. They'd keep their senior pastor, enjoy his talents, and give him his space. Bravo! Would that other organizations understood brain function and helped their employees to succeed. It's definitely different strokes for different folks, and we need all types to make for a successful community.

They're everywhere

It's not just pastors. Similar stories are rumored about famous actors and actresses. On stage or in front of the camera, these often highly introverted individuals are outgoing, clownish, and brilliant with repartee. Backstage they are loners. Take Johnny Carson, for example. When he retired he disappeared! Gone! Others with highly introverted brains choose to live in seclusion (some on tiny islands) and interact with the outside world only as absolutely necessary for their profession. How they are misunderstood! How often their adoring public rakes them over the proverbial coals when requests for autographs and interviews are ignored, avoided, or declined less than gracefully.

Kurt Vonnegut's short story, "Who Am I This Time?" illustrates the special giftedness of an extreme introvert, Harry Nash, who could not even hold a decent conversation with people he had known forever. However, acting on stage for community theater productions, he could powerfully assume almost any role: Abraham Lincoln, Julius Caesar, Cyrano de Bergerac, as he became the person he was impersonating. But when the play was over, even before the bows, Harry was gone.

One high school drama coach remarked that she used to invite the outgoing, extroverted students to try out for plays. She assumed they were the ones who would naturally have a bent for being out in front. Instead, she discovered that many of those kids were absolutely terrified to be on stage. One day, strictly by accident, she mentioned to a very shy junior that he might want to try out for the upcoming play, "The Importance of Being Ernest". Surprisingly, he said, "Okay." At tryouts he shocked everybody, including himself, with an amazing interpretation—and was given the lead. At the performance he knocked everyone's socks off! But after the performance, when it was time for punch and cookies, the actor was nowhere to be found.

Sensitive or Callused

Think back to individuals you have known who likely had extremely introverted brains. Did they appear to be highly or overly sensitive? Were you afraid to hurt their feelings?

Conversely, think of those you've known who likely had extremely extroverted brains. At school, at home, even at work you can do everything short of saying, "Sit still and shut up!" and nothing slows them down. They are so busy searching for the stimulation their brains crave that they may not stop to think about the consequences of their actions. Why do you think they go for the laughs and the attention? More stimulation!

Think of the extremely extroverted brain as having a metaphorical callus that protects it from being readily hurt or bested in highly stimulating, competitive, or combative situations. Individuals with this type of callus thrive in scenarios that could decimate brains that don't possess such a callus. Think of this brain callus as similar to the calluses that carpenters develop to protect their skin from slivers, or that string players develop on their fingers to allow them to play music without pain.

For extremely introverted brains, however, there is no such callus. Too much stimulation, and they become overloaded quickly. They may get hurt, feel pain, or shut down, often by distancing themselves from the environment that contains far too much stimulation.

Literary Link...

> Porcupine was the nickname I gave this chestnut burr, and thought it very appropriate.
> —Natsume Soseki, *Botchan*

This is like the proverbial "people are eggs" idea. Some extreme introverts withdraw from the group, even if they run the risk of being labeled stuck-up, because being alone is safer than being teased, laughed at, or pushed to participate—especially when competition is involved. Have you ever asked someone to play a game of table tennis with you, and the first thing out of their mouth was, "Do we have to keep score?" Likely an extreme introvert! Have you suggested just playing for fun, and an extreme extrovert said, "Why bother playing if we're not going to keep score?" Different responses to a similar situation. This is neither good or bad, it's just different.

Cats Don't Bark

How much more effective life could be if culture and society stopped putting so much pressure on its members to conform to a one size fits all standard. Being different is okay! After all, we wouldn't expect a cat to bark or a dog to meow.

Speaking of animals, some cats are introverts—

they ignore you, hide under the rocking chair, and turn their backs on the one who feeds them—and yet we love those people-tolerating felines anyway. Some attention-begging dogs are extreme people-lovin' extroverts and we love them anyway. Why is it so much harder to do that with human beings?

Literary Link...

> *"There are those who will call you a recluse—but it is better to listen to your own different drummer than to go through life with a ringing in your ears."*
> —William Safire, On Language

The Challenge
Study to understand the context in which your brain operates most efficiently. Cut some slack to the differences between a brain that tolerates and even craves huge amounts of stimulation versus one that doesn't need or can't tolerate similar levels of stimulation. Notice the changes this can make in your world, personally as well as professionally.

It's all about valuing the uniqueness and giftedness of each individual. Remember that you will likely be much more successful if you identify your approximate position on the EAI Continuum and match the majority of your activities to your brain's own unique need for stimulation or relief from stimulation.

Let's go back to Mrs. Tanner's junior high English student from years ago. When Michael graduated from high school, he didn't leave without contacting his former teacher. He stopped by her room and quietly handed Mrs. Tanner a pencil-written, two-sided note containing more words than he had said aloud in all their time together. It read: "Thanks for letting me be me. Even though I was quiet, I learned a lot. I'm not really as shy as everyone thinks!"

Of course he wasn't shy. No more than the shyness each one of us experiences in a new or unfamiliar situation. He did have an extremely introverted brain, which is an entirely different matter. Now, with studies from advanced brain research available, Mrs. Tanner could have validated this student's giftedness as an extreme introvert with much greater relevance, acceptance, and enthusiasm. Years later she learned that Michael was making his mark as a noted researcher. Hmmm.

We each know individuals who remind us of Dolly and Michael. As you think about people you have met who fall into the category of either extreme extroversion or extreme introversion, you may recall times when you might have misunderstood them. You may even feel reflective, or regretful, about the way in which you responded to them, or ignored them. Most likely you hadn't the least idea of what was actually going on in their respective brains!

Often, with the right touch from a sensitive person, an introvert will exercise rare moments of extroversion. Or perhaps the most glaring extrovert will surprise even best friends with profoundly serious thoughts and feelings. That's also part of the gold and part of the glory.

"For nonconformity the world whips you with its displeasure," wrote Ralph Waldo Emerson in "Self Reliance". Done any whipping lately? Been whipped? In today's world, teachers, parents, neighbors, bosses, co-workers, partners—all of us humans—are not only challenged but also obligated to do away with inappropriate stereotyping.

We do better when we know better. Now we know better. It's high time we started doing better!

CHAPTER FOUR
A Sense in Time Saves Mine

> *"Human beings tend to return to environments in which they feel comfortable—environments that they perceive to be nurturing, validating, and accepting."*
>
> —Arlene Taylor

Finding Your Sensory Preference

Complete the Sensory Preference Assessment that begins on this page. (©1984, 2003 Arlene Taylor, PhD). Even if you think you've identified your sensory preference, you may learn something more about yourself. You may even get a surprise or two.

Read each statement and evaluate it as carefully and honestly as possible. If it applies to you **at least** 75% of the time, place a one (1) on the line next to that statement. If the statement applies **less than** 75% of the time, place a zero (0) on the line.

_____ 1. I am very sensitive to odor, taste, temperature, and texture.

_____ 2. I learn a lot about people from the sound and/or tone of their voice.

_____ 3. I like to control the lighting in my environment (e g., dimmer controls, spotlights, uplights, mood lighting) and it is very important to me.

_____ 4. I can usually recognize objects quite easily by touch in the dark.

_____ 5. Sounds usually catch my attention quickly.

_____ 6. I purchase items primarily based on looks/visual appeal.

_____ 7. I tend to select clothes because they feel good and are comfortable to wear.

_____ 8. When selecting a place to live, the view from my abode is of major concern.

_____ 9. I talk to myself frequently, aloud, under my breath, and/or in whispers.

_____ 10. If purchasing a vehicle, room and comfort are very important considerations.

_____ 11. I keep up with current events by listening to radio news more than by watching television.

_____ 12. I tend to select clothes because they look good/sharp.

_____ 13. I prefer frequent changes in body position and move often.

_____ 14. I avoid wearing clothing that is mismatched in color, pattern, or design.

_____ 15. I would rather listen to an audiocassette or CD than read a book.

_____ 16. I like to keep my vehicle washed, waxed, and looking good.

_____ 17. Others consider me chatty or sometimes say that I talk too much.

_____ 18. I often use expressions such as: "my sense is, that fits, I've got a handle on it".

_____ 19. I prefer a map to receiving verbal or printed directions.

_____ 20. I tend to "hear" the voice of the author when reading a personal email or letter.

_____ 21. I enjoy getting physical exercise (e.g., walking, hiking, cycling, jogging).

_____ 22. Strange noises, rattles, or repetitive sounds in my vehicle or house annoy/worry me.

_____ 23. I like to work out and/or take jazzercise or yoga classes.

_____ 24. When eating, the presentation of the food/ table/environment is very important.

_____ 25. I talk to my pets as I would to close friends.

_____ 26. I learn a lot about people from their appearance.

_____ 27. I'd rather participate in sports than observe others playing.

_____ 28. I use rhyming words to help me remember names, labels, dates, or other facts.

_____ 29. I often see something before I hear, sense, or feel it.

_____ 30. I enjoy soaking in the tub or basking in the warm sunshine.

_____ 31. Jingles and acronyms help me to recall information.

_____ 32. I like to receive and/or give back rubs and massages.

_____ 33. I rarely bump into or stumble over objects that I didn't see.

_____ 34. I enjoy touching and hugging my friends.

_____ 35. I prefer to see people when communicating with them.

_____ 36. I study for exams by verbalizing my notes and/or key points aloud.

_____ 37. When shopping, I want the products to be clearly and attractively displayed.

_____ 38. I repeat new words to myself to help fix them in memory.

_____ 39. I readily learned touch typing for keyboard and/or data entry systems.

_____ 40. I prefer pets that I can watch (e.g., fish in a tank, birds).

_____ 41. I have good physical coordination.

_____ 42. I enjoy humming, whistling, or singing (alone or in a group).

_____ 43. I often say things like: "the light just went on, I see what you mean, looks okay to me".

_____ 44. I often use expressions such as: "sounds right, I hear you, keep your ears open".

_____ 45. I learn a lot about people from their handshakes, hugs, or touch.

_____ 46. A picture or diagram is worth 1000 words.

_____ 47. I often tap my toes or feel like moving my body (e.g., dancing) to music/a beat.

_____ 48. I especially appreciate musical programs or concerts.

_____ 49. I like to hold babies or pets that I can touch, stroke, and cuddle.

_____ 50. I prefer to watch TV/movies/videos as compared to reading the book or a script.

_____ 51. Talk shows and interview programs appeal to me.

_____ 52. I especially enjoy making things with my hands (e.g., carving, sculpturing, woodworking, crocheting, knitting, sewing, finger painting).

_____ 53. I often enjoy verbal discussions including long telephone or ham-radio conversations.

_____ 54. I prefer books/magazines that contain graphs, pictures, or colorful illustrations.

_____ 55. I prefer being outdoors over indoors whenever possible.

_____ 56. I really enjoy looking at photo albums.

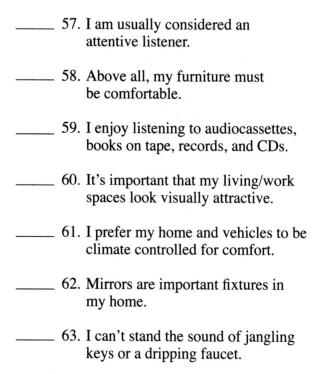

_____ 57. I am usually considered an attentive listener.

_____ 58. Above all, my furniture must be comfortable.

_____ 59. I enjoy listening to audiocassettes, books on tape, records, and CDs.

_____ 60. It's important that my living/work spaces look visually attractive.

_____ 61. I prefer my home and vehicles to be climate controlled for comfort.

_____ 62. Mirrors are important fixtures in my home.

_____ 63. I can't stand the sound of jangling keys or a dripping faucet.

On the next page, write your answers beside the corresponding numbers. When completed, add up the points in each column and write your three scores in the column boxes at the bottom of the page.

2 =	3 =	1 =
5 =	6 =	4 =
9 =	8 =	7 =
11 =	12 =	10 =
15 =	14 =	13 =
17 =	16 =	18 =
20 =	19 =	21 =
22 =	24 =	23 =
25 =	26 =	27 =
28 =	29 =	30 =
31 =	33 =	32 =
36 =	35 =	34 =
38 =	37 =	39 =
42 =	40 =	41 =
44 =	43 =	45 =
48 =	46 =	47 =
51 =	50 =	49 =
53 =	54 =	52 =
57 =	56 =	55 =
59 =	60 =	58 =
63 =	62 =	61 =

Column **A Total**	Column **B Total**	Column **C Total**

Your Preference

Transfer your scores from each column to the appropriate blank below. That will make it easier for you to compare.

Column A _____ **= auditory**

Column B _____ **= visual**

Column C _____ **= kinesthetic**

Which column has the highest score? It likely represents your overall sensory preference.

If two scores are tied, one of those scores may indicate your preference while the other represents skills you developed in order to relate to someone significant in your life. If one of the tied scores is kinesthetic, consider the possibility that your innate preference may be kinesthetic, but you have pulled back from it. Try to identify possible reasons this might have occurred (e.g., our current litigious society makes touching others inadvisable, if not dangerous).

If all scores are equal, recognize that this is not a naturally occurring pattern. Use this clue as an opportunity to evaluate your sensory history. Try to uncover and identify factors that may have influenced you to repress your sensory preference.

Understanding some of the characteristics typically exhibited by individuals based on their sensory preference can help you deal more effectively with others.

Understanding Your Sensory Preference

What gets our attention? Sensory stimuli, the information we absorb through eyes, ears, nose, mouth, and skin. Unless we have a disability in one of the sensory systems (e.g., visually challenged, hearing impaired, altered sense of smell), we have the ability to use all the senses and can process data that comes to the brain in all three systems—visual, auditory, kinesthetic.

However, we may find that we are more aware of one system than another, in specific situations or environments. For example, we may be more aware of our auditory system when attending a concert, of our kinesthetic system while eating holiday dinner with all the trimmings, or of our visual system when visiting an art gallery or traveling to a new country.

Most human beings have a sensory preference—that is, one type of stimuli tends to get our attention faster and register more quickly in our brain. We usually tend to feel more comfortable when we receive sensory data in our preferred system and better understood when we are in an environment that recognizes and respects our sensory preference.

Literary Link...

> *As your senses awaken, all the inlets to the mind are set open.*
> —Cathleen Schine, Rameau's Niece

All There From the Beginning...

As small children, most of us used our senses almost equally, assuming we were unimpaired. The information they brought helped us to learn at rates that probably won't be duplicated at any other time in life. By the age of 5 or 6, the brain usually begins to select a preferred sensory system (although what stimulates this selection isn't well understood).

Gradually, we began to take in information more readily by looking at things, hearing things, or sensing things through touch, taste, and smell. That preference probably won't change much in adulthood, unless we were shamed or abused during childhood in a way that prompted us to repress, deny, or ignore our sensory preference.

We communicate with others through the sensory systems. Simply by understanding more about these systems and becoming more aware of our preference as compared to that of others, we can enhance all our relationships.

Matching Actions to Preference

Let's say your daughter has gone away to college in another state, and you want to communicate how much you love her and miss her. If she has a visual preference, you might send her a gift for her dormitory room—a green plant, picture, poster, or flower arrangement. Remember to tell her how beautiful she is, or how much you like the décor in her room, how much you miss seeing her around the house.

If she's an auditory girl, you could send her a CD, windchimes, or an e-mail greeting card.

Tell her you look forward to hearing the sound of her voice, and give her a calling card so she can phone you!

If kinesthetic, your daughter might enjoy a cuddly teddy bear, a soft quilt or feather pillow, scented candles, or potpourri. When you're together, give her a hug or treat her to her favorite kinesthetic activity—tennis, a massage, swimming, or hiking. Similar types of sensory-matched gift ideas can work equally well for your spouse, partner, or best friend. Learning about sensory preferences can empower you as an individual, and it can also extend beneficially into your family, school, social, church, and work worlds.

Literary Link...

> *If I read a book and it makes my body so cold no fire can warm me, I know that is poetry. If I feel physically as if the top of my head were taken off, I know that is poetry. These are the only ways I know it. Is there any other way?*
> —Emily Dickinson

Your Brain and the Senses

Even though sensory stimuli can enter through any part of the body, including nerves that flow through the brain stem, the decoding centers are believed to be located in the thinking brain. In adulthood, sensory preference is believed to occur in the general population in approximately a 60-20-20 distribution among visuals, auditories, and kinesthetics.

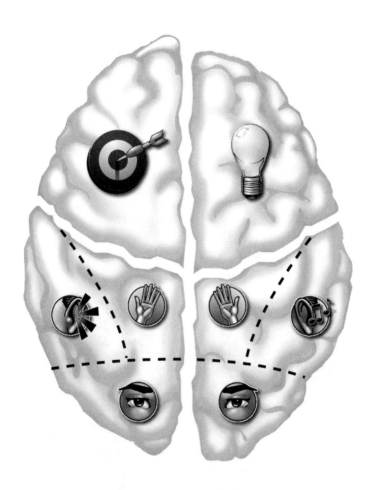

The Thinking Brain

Brain Bits...

All sensory stimuli can be powerful, but odors can trigger memories faster than any other type, especially odors associated with emotion. For example, your home may include these smells: coffee, chocolate chip cookies, apple pie, your dad's pipe, fresh lilacs in the spring, or vanilla-scented candles.

In fact, your nose is just a synapse away from your emotional brain where incoming sensory information is forwarded to higher centers of association in the thinking brain. Negative memories can also be triggered by odors: smoke, alcohol, dirty diapers, a musty basement, pollution, disease, or sour milk.

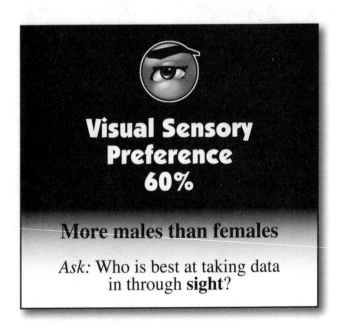

Visual Sensory Preference 60%

More males than females

Ask: Who is best at taking data in through **sight**?

Auditory
Sensory Preference
20%

More females than males

Ask: Who is best at taking data in through **sound**?

Kinesthetic Sensory
Preference
20%

Equal females and males

Ask: Who is best at taking data in via **taste**, **touch**, **smell** and **body position**?

Brain Bits...

> Decoding centers in the thinking brain for the sensory systems can receive and process up to ten million bits of data per second.

Synesthesia

The term Synesthesia applies to an interesting neurological phenomenon where the senses blend (coordinate and overlap) in an unusual manner. For example, a person may hear colors and see or taste sounds. Approximately 1 person in 100,000 has profound synesthesia—more heightened in highly creative people and associated with incredible powers of memory.

There is an interesting religious song written and sung by Chris Rice entitled, "Smell the Color Nine," which ties the idea of finding God to smelling colors: "But sometimes finding You, is just like trying to smell the color nine."

I don't know if you've found God, but I'm quite sure that some folks have smelled the color 9!

Hallucinations

Hallucinations have always been a hot topic, at least in some environments. The movie, "A Beautiful Mind", has gone a long way toward helping people understand how real these altered sensory experiences can be.

Hallucinations can be described as intense, self-generated experiences involving one or more of the senses. Sometimes they can result from the misrouting of sensory data to the wrong decoding center. For example, studies show that the voices heard by individuals diagnosed with schizophrenia are usually their own. Speech, generated in one portion of the brain, is experienced as hearing in another portion.

Hallucinations can also be the result of giftedness. For example, an individual with a photographic memory is more likely to experience hallucinations.

Children who play with invisible playmates may actually be seeing those playmates as clearly as the rest of us see real people. One mother told of her little boy having created six imaginary (to her) brothers whom he named and talked about regularly. And they could fly! How silly, you might think. And then again...why not? Just because most adults have lost their colorful imaginations doesn't mean children need to.

Literary Link...

> *Zorba scratched his head [and said]: "I've got a thick skull boss. I don't grasp these things easily. Ah, if only you could dance all that you've just said, then I'd understand...Or if you could tell me all that in a story, boss."*
> —Kazantzakis

Characteristics of a Visual Sensory Preference

Individuals with a visual sensory preference may:

- Use visual words and metaphors (e.g., I see. Picture this. The light just went on. It's crystal clear to me. She talked until she was blue in the face. Do you see what I mean?)

- Have a higher-pitched voice

- Tend to speak rapidly

- Breathe shallowly or hold breath at times while thinking

- Draw pictures in the air with arms and hands

- React faster and more intensely to visual stimuli

- Like pets that are interesting to watch

- Prefer colorful environments and work spaces

- Want food to look appealing and attractive (may dislike beets and mashed potatoes blending together on a plate)

- Have been afraid of the dark or feared scary movies, pictures as a child

- Believe that the way things look is extremely important

- Pick up on the facial expressions of others

- Be hurt or irritated by lack of eye contact

- Learn most quickly by seeing how something is done

Characteristics of an Auditory Sensory Preference

Individuals with an auditory sensory preference tend to:

- Use auditory words and metaphors (e.g., That sounds okay to me. It's clear as a bell. Keep your ear to the ground. That doesn't ring true. Do you hear what I mean?)

- Exhale deeply and sigh, especially when tired, tense, or stressed

- Cock head to one side when listening carefully or speaking intensely, or cup or touch ears

- React faster and/or more intensely to auditory stimuli (e.g., sirens, bells, whistles)

- Like pets that make sounds or talk

- Prefer toys that make sounds

- Want food to sound right (e.g., may like or dislike the crunchy sounds)

- Have been frightened by loud/scary sounds (e.g., thunder, crying, fireworks) as a child

- Pay attention to the sound of clothing (e.g., like/dislike swishing of nylon or clanking of zippers)

- Be sensitive to things they hear in the environment (e.g., arguing, yelling, whispering, discordant sounds)

- Feel nurtured/loved quickly by positive sounds (e.g., kind words, in nature, music, friendly voices)

- Be hurt by lack of positive auditory input (e.g., silent treatment, harsh voices, unpleasant noises)

- Learn most quickly by hearing how something is done through verbal explanations or by written instructions

Characteristics of a Kinesthetic Sensory Preference

Individuals with a kinesthetic sensory preference (taste, odor, touch, position sense) are generally those who:

- Use kinesthetic words and metaphors (e.g., That doesn't fit. That doesn't feel right. I've got a gut feeling.... I'm trying to get in touch with that idea. Let's hammer out a plan. It's as clear as mud. Spare me from the jolting headlines!)

- Have low-pitched voices

- Tend to breathe deeply and speak slowly

- Prefer to work with their hands

- React faster and/or more intensely to kinesthetic stimuli

- Like pets that are comfortable to touch and are often intuitive with animals

- As a child preferred toys that felt good (e.g., smooth, soft, interesting texture)

- Want food to feel right (e.g., not too hot or cold, not slimy or scratchy) and be tasty (e.g., often lean toward the gourmet)

- May be afraid of pain, physical irritations, or discomfort

- Need their clothing to feel right and not be restrictive, rough, or too hot or too cold (Don't purchase clothes for a kinesthetic. Just give them a gift certificate so they can make their own selection or they may never wear the item.)

- Are sensitive to environmental conditions (e.g., temperature, drafts, furniture texture)

- May be hurt by a lack of touch or harsh touch (e.g., spanked, kicked, jerked, hair pulled, held down and tickled)

- Often learn most quickly by actually touching and doing. Hands-on style.

Literary Link...

My taste buds experienced a violent ecstasy. A whole opera of sensations rolled off my tongue.
— Henri Troyat, after tasting a coffee ice cream sundae for the first time (quoted in The New York Times 7-22-92)

Knowing Your Sensory Preference

Your sensory preference impacts the way you learn, because it is generally easier to assimilate information that comes to you in your sensory preference. Conversely, it can be more difficult to absorb information that comes to you in a non-preferred sensory system. Although usually you can do so, it can be much more energy-intensive, it will be harder to transfer data to your long-term memory banks, or recall it later.

Differences in sensory preference underlie many communication problems, situational misunderstandings, and feelings of discomfort. Being aware of this can help you prevent some of these from occurring, whether it involves interactions between parents and children, teachers and students, ministers and congregations, employers and employees, or professional/romantic partnerships.

Romantic Situations

Romantic activities tend to activate all three sensory systems. During courtship partners usually talk to each other, listen, and express affection verbally. They take pains to show each other a good time. They may look at each other in that special way and affirm each other's appearance. They touch and hug and kiss. It's easy to see why being on the receiving end of this level of sensory stimuli can make one want to spend the rest of his/her life with the nurturer.

In business, contacts often wine and dine each other, perhaps take trips to view the property or institution, and often provide gifts or incentives to spur the negotiations. All things being equal, this type of whole-brain interaction is designed to encourage an individual to look with favor upon the proposed partnership or merger.

Unfortunately, this level of sensory nurturing tends to fall off when the goal of the courtship has been reached or when the contract is signed on the dotted line. If their sensory preferences do not match, before much time passes, the individuals may experience some level of discomfort or discontent and not understand why. It could very well be that because their sensory preferences differ, each eventually begins relating to the other in his/her own sensory preference. Since they don't match, the sensory stimuli don't register quickly in the brain.

For example, the visual person may dress and groom carefully, give gifts that are lovely to look at, and take the partner places to see things. But the visual may not talk enough to please the auditory partner, or may fail to offer sufficient nonsexual touch to help meet the partner's skin-hunger needs.

The auditory person may talk of love, but neglect to look at the other person in that special way, may fail to groom the self carefully, may overlook the planning of outings, or fail to touch or hug appropriately. Remember Neil Diamond's song, "You Don't Bring Me Flowers Any More"? —Sung like a true visual!

The kinesthetic partner may be good at touching ("I Wanna Hold Your Haaaannnnd"), yet may neglect attentions that would appeal to a visual or an auditory person, such as verbal communication, listening, giving gifts, and calling often.

If partners match in their sensory preference, each usually feels nurtured as preferred stimuli register quickly in his/her brain. But, if the couple's sensory preferences don't match, then sensory preference needs to be understood so partners can affirm each other effectively. After all, the goal is for each person to stay feeling desired and loved.

An easy way to be sure all the bases are covered is to identify each other's sensory preference and offer nurturing every day in your partner's preference. (This isn't as hard as it sounds if you're alert and are aware of sensory signals.) Or, you could just continue to relate to each other in a whole-brained manner. In other words, just do it all!

Tactics for the Work Place

A courtship situation can involve romance, but it can also be a business courtship situation, as well. Let's analyze an example.

George's Story

George is a very successful real estate agent. When others in sales are moaning and groaning about the flat market, he regularly manages to connect buyers with sellers. Why? Because he understands the sensory systems!

When homebuyers first enter George's office, he asks them to describe exactly what they want in a home. He watches their body language, listens for words and phrases they use, and tries to sense their motivation. Then he matches his sales pitch to their sensory preference.

For example, if buyers appear to be visual, he may tell them that the house possesses eye appeal and that there are windows overlooking breath-taking views. He asks them to notice the fine craftsmanship, from the carving on the doors to the trim over the portico.

To tap into the auditory system, George may talk about the house being soundly constructed, mentioning the excellent insulation to block out undesirable sounds, or calling their attention to the rustling of leaves on the trees surrounding the property. He would, as appropriate, point out the babbling brook nearby or birds in the bushes, happy sounds of school children from a nearby school, or even the quietude in a country setting.

If George is addressing the kinesthetic system, he'll draw the clients' attention to the fine finishing detail and plush carpets. He may suggest that they touch the wood on the railing or the marble on the countertops. He may point out that the way in which the kitchen window is positioned allows the warmth of the sun to permeate the room. He may talk about the potential for sitting on the wide patio to soak up the perfume from wildflowers growing in the lot next door, or how they will enjoy the raspberries on the bushes near the fence. He may also suggest that the porch would be an ideal location for a swing.

And when George isn't sure which of the three sensory systems is most appropriate, he addresses all three in his presentation. Some of his colleagues poke fun at the "scientific" way in which he approaches sales. (Actually, they're a bit jealous!) They accuse him of using manipulation. George says he just understands what works for the brain and presents housing options in a language his customers can understand. And people love to buy from George. Some of his colleagues are starting to get on board, as well. After all, you can't argue with success!

Victoria's Story

Victoria, a health counselor, uses a similar approach when working with patients who need to regain their health through lifestyle changes. She is a health counselor. When encouraging smokers to quit, she helps individuals with an auditory preference understand how nice it will be not to hear themselves wheezing and gasping for air when they climb stairs or exercise. She reminds visuals how great it will be to avoid nicotine stains and burn holes on their clothing. She suggests that kinesthetics will enhance their tasting ability, to say nothing of having nicer breath for sweeter kissing! It works!

Endless Potential

If you do any public speaking, addressing all three sensory preferences can increase the likelihood that your audience will stay tuned in to your presentation. By connecting to all sensory systems—through stories, word pictures, tangible objects, multimedia, overheads, Power Point presentations, and handouts—you can engage your listeners at deeper levels.

If your child isn't doing well in school, check to see if his/her sensory preference is in the minority, or if it is different from that of the teacher's. Hmmm.

Career Choices

Your sensory preference can impact not only the career path toward which you gravitate, but also your situational comfort level while trying to complete key tasks. Following are examples of some career paths that might be favored by individuals based on their sensory preference.

Visual Preference

Airline pilots
Fire fighters
Sharp shooters, marksmen
Entertainers (TV, movies, videos)
Artisans
Designers
Models
Sign-language translators
Tasks that require marked visual acuity
(e.g., traffic controllers)

Auditory Preference

Musicians
Psychotherapists, Counselors
Speech Therapists
Hosts of talk shows, radio broadcasters
Public speakers
Readers
Telephone communicators
Foreign Language translators
Voice-over specialists

Kinesthetic Preference

Athletes
Dancers
Surgeons
Masseuse/masseur
Mechanics
Computer programmers, designers
Artists (especially art forms that use the
hands in the process)
Physical Therapists
Occupational Therapists

Challenges in Today's Hands-Off Society...

Every human being has skin-hunger needs. In order to thrive, we require non-sexual, physical touch affirmation. Unfortunately, many people don't get enough touch validation. And in today's somewhat "no-touch" society, individuals with a kinesthetic sensory preference often suffer the most deprivation, and have the most difficulty getting their skin-hunger needs met adequately. Cultural prohibitions against touching contribute to this. Consequently, many people (males especially) are touch-deprived.

Some males are fortunate to have friends or a partner with whom they can exchange touch. Others have pets to handle. Still others try to satisfy their touching needs through sexual activity. It is critically important for a person with a kinesthetic preference to take positive steps toward obtaining nonsexual, physical-touch. If that person is you, teach your friends to give you nonsexual touch (the type of touch that helps meet skin-hunger needs). Allot time to spend with animals that like to be touched, curl up with a soft afghan and a stuffed animal, or soak in the tub amidst your favorite candle fragrances. Make life work for you!

All children require nonsexual touch affirmation just to stay alive. Studies of infants in orphanages showed that without sufficient touch, the babies died. When elderly volunteers were recruited to simply hold the babies on an average of fifteen minutes per day, the infants stopped dying. Amazing! Children with a kinesthetic preference need touch even more because that type of sensory stimuli registers most quickly in their brains. Children who do not get their touch needs met appropriately may fail to thrive or learn, may be more vulnerable to inappropriate touch (e.g., physical or sexual abuse), or may be at a higher risk for unwed pregnancies.

Individuals with a kinesthetic preference often present a challenging paradox. Although they generally relate to the world through touch, taste, smell, position/posture, and sensitivity to the environment, they can also be extremely discriminating about who touches them. Be aware of this and try to avoid bruising kinesthetics through unwelcome, intrusive, or insensitive touch.

Again, if this is you, learn to communicate kindly and firmly the type of touch you desire or are willing to tolerate. It's your brain, your sensory preference, and you understand it best!

People Like to Feel Real

One evening a family decided to go out for dinner at their favorite restaurant. They were shown to a table that overlooked the bay, and within minutes the waitress arrived to take their order. She began with the father and asked each member in turn what he or she wanted. Finally reaching the youngest member of the family, the waitress asked, "And what would you like to eat, young lady?"

"A burger and fries," the little girl answered politely.
"Bring her lasagna," said the mother.
"And what would you like to drink?" the waitress continued.

"7-Up, please," the child replied.

"Bring her lasagna and milk," the mother said firmly. The waitress looked from the mother to the little girl, back to the mother, and then wrote down the order.

In due time, the food arrived. To the delight of the wee customer, and the consternation of her mother, the waitress placed a burger, fries, and 7-Up in front of the little girl.

The child looked at her plate. Eyes glowing with excitement, she fairly shouted in a voice that carried to the far corners of the restaurant, "Mommy, Mommy! That lady thinks I'm real!"

Increase Your Awareness

Are you aware of sensory preference? Your own, as well as that of others? Do you use the sensory systems by design to help the people around you feel real? Paying attention to the sensory systems is important. Do something often for your partner (children, friends, or co-workers) in their sensory preference and watch your relationships with them improve.

If you can learn to recognize and graciously accept nurturing from others, even when it doesn't come in your preferred style, you are a most wise individual. Other people may try to affirm you using activities or strategies that match their sensory preference. If you fail to recognize, acknowledge, or accept their affirmation just because it didn't come to you in your sensory preference, you may miss a great deal of nurturing. Don't miss out on a blessing because it isn't packaged the way you expect.

Tips for Enhancing Your Sensory Skills

Communication and behavior that acknowledge and nurture sensory preference is learned. Here are some tips to consider:

- **Knowledge:** Identify your own sensory preference and then be alert to situations that could be enhanced through applying what you know.

- **Choice:** Choose to practice whole-brain-nurturing behaviors whenever possible (e.g., when greeting others look them in the eye, shake hands, and say something verbally).

- **Competency:** Develop skills in all three sensory systems. That way you will be ready for almost any type of situation.

- **Creativity:** Be innovative in using the sensory systems. Try something new when nurturing others. Avoid doing the same thing over and over again, or believing that simply because something worked once it will work for all the time.

- **Implementation:** Communicate with others in their sensory preference. Do something every day for your close friends/family members in their sensory preference. The sensory stimuli will register quickly and easily in their brains and will help them feel comfortable and affirmed. When in doubt, use all three!

The myth has always been: Seeing is believing. But the fact is: No, sometimes we believe through hearing certain sounds or receiving touch.

In Shel Silverstein's popular poetry book, *Where the Sidewalk Ends*, we are gently reminded about the impact of sharing love. The picture shows a forlorn little human being holding a poster on which is written the letter "V." The verse reads:

> Ricky was "L", but
> he's home with the flu,
> Lizzie, "O," had some
> homework to do,
> Mitchell, "E" prob'ly
> got lost on the way,
> So I'm all the love
> that could make it today.

Appropriate Sensory Communication

If no one else is around to do it, if no one else is around who understands it, the job could just become yours. Use sensory stimuli by design rather than default. Make a positive difference in someone's life. It might even be your own!

CHAPTER FIVE
Your Brain Has a Bent
(Not a Dent)

An ulcer, gentlemen, is an unkissed imagination taking its revenge for having been jilted. It is an unwritten poem, an undanced dance, an unpainted watercolor. It is a declaration... that a clear spring of joy has not been tapped.
—John Ciardi, addressing Canadian businessmen, 1952

Your brain is as unique as your thumbprint. This means that some activities may require higher expenditures of energy as compared to other brains. The reverse is also true. Some activities may require less! Understanding more about the amounts of energy your brain uses in your own thinking process and aligning your choices, insofar as possible, to what your brain does easily, can add life to your years, and maybe years to your life!

This concept can be compared to getting a smoother ride in a car when the driver understands how that car's transmission works most effectively, or to making sure that the manufacturer-specified fuel is used in the vehicle.

In a similar way, each brain possesses some built-in advantages that result in one's own innate giftedness or personal brain bent. When you understand these advantages and work with them instead of against them, your brain can function more efficiently and effectively. You're in for a smoother ride through life. You usually have more fun, too. (And we're all for that!)

John's Story

John, a college sophomore noted for his math skills, was selected by the math chair to be a peer tutor for struggling non-math majors. Although he acknowledged the honor of being selected, John didn't look forward to the job. "I don't like explaining math concepts," he said. "I'd rather be a lab assistant in the science department." After two months in the math center, he quit— burned out, but fearing he had disappointed his professors.

Jeannie's Story

Jeannie had worked for 11 years as a supervisor in the billing department of a large teaching hospital. While competent at her job to all external appearances, privately she was experiencing burnout, suffering from depression, and gaining weight. Several times she spoke with her boss about applying for another position as postings showed up on the "job's available" board. Each time, Jeannie allowed herself to be talked out of applying because "she was so valuable to the billing department." When her physician wanted to prescribe medication for Jeannie's worsening depression, she decided to interview for the position of Director of Volunteer Services. She was hired and within three months even her former co-workers could recognize that this position was a "great fit."

Literary Link...

A human being should live only in harmony with his very own nature and according to his very own nature. He should live in accordance with the truth about himself.

—Carl Jung

Warren's Story

Warren's mechanical abilities were known in five counties. He had a natural knack for finding problems in cars and fixing them reasonably and quickly, and he made big bucks doing just that. However, his first love was teaching. Working on cars bored him, while teaching novice mechanics absolutely energized him. Warren tried to convince his dealership to let him work at the training institute, but they insisted that he couldn't be replaced in the garage.

What these three individuals wanted to do, versus what they were told to do, demonstrates the concept of wanting to work within one's own natural preference. They might not have known that technically, but their brains were telling them where they belonged.

Preference is an Advantage

Thinking process preference can be thought of in several ways: as an order of choice, as the power of choosing, and as a biochemical advantage. In relation to brain function, preference describes the ability of the brain to complete some activities with less energy expenditure than is required for other activities. Left to its own devices (all things being equal), the brain would likely gravitate toward the first type of activities. When you engage in activities that match your brain's biochemical advantage, you can generally expect to attain a higher level of competence in those skills (given sufficient practice), engage in them with lower expenditures of energy, do them more easily, and experience higher levels of enjoyment and fulfillment.

Brain Bent is Built In

That's right, your brain bent came with your birth package. It began to develop during gestation. As Daniel Seigel put it, "The left and right sides of the brain have distinct circuits that become predominant early in life, even in the embryo."

By an early age, if you were exposed to a variety of activities, and were encouraged in the areas you enjoyed, your own brain bent began to surface. That's why gymnastics and music lessons, T-ball and chess, golf and art classes (in balance, of course) can help the brain to develop, even though these activities can keep caregivers running. During those exposures, some focuses are weeded out, while others can get serious and become intentional.

And books! Surround children with books. Studies show that children who are read to usually like to read. Have books in the playroom, bathroom, car, family room, tree house, and kitchen. Everywhere!

What sometimes happens is that parents/caregivers offer experiences that match their preferences rather than offering a range of activities, some of which may better match the preferences of the individual child. It's important to expose children to variety while recognizing and encouraging their preferences. Following one's natural brain bent is much easier and more fun. It shapes our ultimate success in life.

Development of natural brain bent in a child can be sidetracked if high levels of anxiety exist in the family system or in that of the child's culture/society. If parents and caregivers are calm and possess a neutral, open position with the child, brain bent can blossom.

Pablo's Story

As a little guy, artist Pablo Picasso wanted to scribble all over everything. So his mother gave him pencils and colors and encouraged him to try. By age seven he was drawing pictures, following his brain bent to produce the incredible art treasures of later life. What if his mother had insisted he play with tools? A violin? A fishing pole?

Clearly, there is a huge difference between having learned to do something well and doing it easily. It is the difference between the feeling that you're playing—or working. Washing and waxing a car could be fun to one person, drudgery to the next. The same with cooking a gourmet meal or playing an instrument. Torture or treat—it's all about brain bent.

Anatomy of Brain Bent

Important to your understanding your brain's preference is the knowledge of a few basic anatomical details. The human brain is composed of many parts. Some of these were mentioned in Chapter One. Your cerebrum—or thinking brain—is composed of eight lobes that are grouped into four divisions by natural fissures.

Brain Bits...

The thinking brain is divided by natural fissures into four cerebral divisions.

According to Benziger, each of these four cerebral divisions has its own built-in scanner. Each perceives the environment somewhat differently and focuses on specific interests. Stretching the metaphor just a bit, one could say that each is a specialist in its own field. Think of each as having a purpose and containing functions that can help you manage specific situations in life.

The two frontal lobes are believed to contain executive functions that enable us to plan, set goals, prioritize our actions, manage willpower, envision and make changes, and develop/access conscience. The other six lobes, located behind and slightly below the two frontal lobes, are thought to contain decoding centers for sensory stimuli (visual, auditory, and kinesthetic), in addition to a whole range of other functions. The three lobes on the left side contain functions that help us to develop habits and follow routines accurately. Those on the right side contain functions related to natural musical ability, attaining peace and harmony, and building spiritual connections.

Examples of frontal lobes functions

(although there may be some overlap)

Functions of the **left frontal** lobe can help us develop skills related to:

- Setting and achieving goals
- Making timely and objective decisions
- Engaging in inductive/deductive reasoning
- Abstracting and analyzing data
- Managing willpower, including setting personal boundaries
- Developing and utilizing conscience

Examples of posterior lobes functions

(although there may be some overlap)

Functions of the **left posterior** lobes can help us develop skills related to:

- Developing and following routines accurately
- Implementing activities of self-care
- Honoring and following traditions
- Learning the rules and following them
- Maintaining the status quo
- Providing services that are necessary to life in our society (e.g., activities connected with any service industry)

Functions of the **right frontal** lobe can help us develop skills related to:

- Envisioning, anticipating, and making changes
- Identifying patterns, trends, and the context
- Absorbing the big picture
- Daydreaming/brainstorming
- Risking doing something in a new way/innovating
- Spontaneity and a sense of humor

Functions of the **right posterior** lobes can help us develop skills related to:

- Promoting connectedness with others and with nature
- Processing spiritual experiences
- Reading nonverbal body language
- Recognize faces and storing emotional memories
- Celebrating
- Pursuing harmony (e.g., among sounds, colors, and shapes; with people, nature, and the environment)

Energy Expenditure

PET Scan studies have shown that the brain works many times harder when performing tasks that don't match its own bent. Working harder means an increased metabolic rate, along with higher needs for oxygen, glucose, micronutrients, and rest.

Activities that match your own innate giftedness—your advantage or bent—utilize much less energy. Remember, bent rhymes with dent, and whether or not you follow your brain bent can result in a smaller or larger dent in your energy bank.

Your brain knows how it functions most effectively. It wants you to figure this out, too. It tries in myriad ways to get your attention as you engage in life's activities.

Sometimes it "drags its feet" and pushes you to procrastinate. Sometimes it tempts you to do favorite activities when you're really expected— or scheduled—to do something else. Sometimes it gives you a little euphoric burst of energy, or conversely, allows you to get sick. The secret is to pay attention as your brain tries to communicate with you.

How to Get Started

Figuring out your own brain bent is a bit like solving a puzzle—your puzzle. You might begin by asking yourself several questions:

- What types of activities do I find fun, easy, and energizing?

- What types of activities do I find frustrating, difficult, and exhausting?

- What types of activities are somewhat neutral in terms of pleasure, dislike, or energy expenditure?

Once you have a general picture, it's time to get more specific and analyze activities or tasks individually. Begin by jotting down a dozen activities—tasks that you do, or are supposed to do, on a regular basis. You may find it helpful to begin with your home life first, then move on to your work life.

Make sure the activities you select to analyze require active mental picturing versus passive mental picturing. What's the difference? Active mental picturing is necessary for all types of creativity, problem solving, and brainstorming. Here your brain is actively functioning to accomplish something. Building an object with a set of blocks or Legos® requires the brain to actively design and create.

Passive mental picturing means that your brain is processing what another brain has already actively created. Watching television, for example, is usually more of a passive mental picturing activity. You're observing what others are doing rather than performing the activity yourself. Using passive mental picturing some of the time isn't bad. We all do it and it's good we can, but it doesn't challenge the brain and grow dendrites (projections on the neuron much like fingers on a hand) in the way that active mental picturing does.

Activity Evaluation

Read over the following list of activities. Choose twelve activites that best describe your day-to-day life.

Remember that we have a work life regardless of the labels applied to what we do—housewife, childcare worker, truck driver, commodities broker, sailor, shoemaker, or candlestick maker—whether or not we receive a salary. There's nothing magic about these activites. They are simply tools to help you evaluate the activities in your life. However, if you are honest about evaluating your personal and work tasks, a pattern will begin to emerge.

Activities

1. I analyze financial statements
2. I give speeches
3. I build "sets" (theatre groups, t.v., video, etc.)
4. I rebuild engines
5. I compile, file, and maintain records
6. I negotiate contracts
7. I repair electronic or mechanical equipment
8. I fish/hunt using precision equipment
9. I read books/articles by experts
10. I compose popular melodies
11. I perform solo dance routines
12. I design new products
13. I visit museums and/or art galleries
14. I prepare food dishes rarely using a recipe
15. I sculpt objects
16. I carve objects
17. I take food orders at a restaurant
18. I prepare my own taxes
19. I shop for groceries
20. I do the laundry
21. I fill the car with fuel
22. I play cards
23. I solve cross-word puzzles regularly
24. I balance my checkbook
25. I collect and organize (e.g., stamps, coins)
26. I assemble models (e.g., cars, ships, planes)
27. I perform routine administrative duties
28. I cook food following a recipe
29. I do peer counseling (e.g., grief recovery)
30. I sing in a local choir

31. I play an instrument in a band
32. I play an instrument with a symphony
33. I perform in a repertoire group
34. I dance in a troupe
35. I listen to individuals tell me their troubles
36. I give a party to celebrate almost anything
37. I write romantic short stories
38. I accompany a choral group on the piano
39. I give dinner parties at my home
40. I answer the telephone for the crisis hot line
41. I reshelve books at the library
42. I write poetry
43. I cater food for large dinner parties
44. I ride roller coasters
45. I picket for causes
46. I give massages
47. I walk/run on a treadmill
48. I ride a bicycle
49. I hike
50. I swim
51. I read x-ray films
52. I clean teeth in a dental office
53. I iron
54. I clean the bathrooms
55. I vacuum the house
56. I wash/wax floors
57. I clean the kitchen
58. I mow the lawn
59. I clean the garage
60. I wash/wax/vacuum the car

61. I greet people at church
62. I wash dishes by hand
63. I load/unload the dishwasher
64. I weed the garden/flowerbed
65. I proofread written material
66. I bathe the dog/cat
67. I make clothing alterations
68. I decorate cakes
69. I design patterns for clothing
70. I cut out and sew blouses (etc.)
71. I babysit toddlers
72. I change the oil in my car
73. I change/rotate the tires on my car
74. I play computer games
75. I put together jigsaw puzzles
76. I style hair
77. I groom dogs
78. I create flower arrangements
79. I index and alphabetize files
80. I make travel arrangements
81. I take minutes for board/committee meetings
82. I open mail for the boss
83. I compose business letters
84. I deliver packages/mail
85. I transcribe medical/legal dictation
86. I read water meters and record data
87. I schedule appointments
88. I process insurance claims
89. I do patient billing
90. I research legal cases

91. I sing/read to the elderly at a nursing home
92. I serve food to the homeless
93. I shovel snow
94. I drive a school bus
95. I inspect meat at a packing plant
96. I pet animals at the petting zoo
97. I repair appliances
98. I repair plumbing leaks
99. I repair roofing leaks
100. I drive an emergency vehicle
101. I enhance digital photographs
102. I transcribe court proceedings
103. I prepare investigative reports
104. I anchor the news on television
105. I host a radio talk show
106. I cashier at a store
107. I clean swimming pools
108. I change bed linen in hotel rooms
109. I take telephone reservations
110. I screen phone calls for my boss
111. I operate heavy equipment
112. I sell clothing
113. I write parking tickets
114. I find directions by reading maps
115. I keep records of my own expenses
116. I organize and set up files
117. I work on an assembly line
118. I service office machines (e.g., copiers)
119. I do bookkeeping
120. I audit accounts

121. I counsel high school students about careers
122. I argue cases in court
123. I invent new products
124. I negotiate automobile sales
125. I sell life insurance
126. I sell pharmaceutical products
127. I fill orders for merchandise
128. I deliver lumber
129. I register patients
130. I greet and seat patrons at a restaurant
131. I make public presentations
132. I write response letters for complaints
133. I direct a choir
134. I make sales calls
135. I chair a social committee
136. I serve as master of ceremonies
137. I solicit funds
138. I teach a class at church/synagogue
139. I teach mathematics
140. I teach biology
141. I correct exam papers for my professor
142. I teach creative writing
143. I teach auto-mechanics
144. I teach cooking classes
145. I estimate repair costs (automotive services)
146. I do keyboarding and data entry
147. I go surfboarding for recreation
148. I surfboard competitively
149. I play a musical instrument
150. I perform with a local drama group

151. I write articles for the newspaper

152. I compose popular songs

153. I paint watercolor scenes

154. I put out oil-well fires

155. I play golf for recreation

156. I play golf in tournaments

158. I white-water raft

159. I follow an 8-5 routine

160. I set my own hours on the job

Completing the Evaluation

After choosing twelve activities from the list (or coming up with your own) fill in the activity blanks provided at the top of each page.

After you have filled in the activity blanks, carefully read the fifteen evaluation statements under each activity. Choose and mark the five statements that best describe how the activity affects you.

An example activity and evaluation has been completed for you.

When you finish marking the best five statements for all twelve activites, turn to page 152 for instructions on how to score the results.

Activity #1 (Example)

I REPAIR ELECTRONIC OR MECHANICAL EQUIPMENT.

_____ 1. I find that time drags by when doing it

X 2. I enjoy doing it

_____ 3. I would prefer to delegate or hire it out if possible

_____ 4. I dread doing it but must do it, or believe/ have been taught that I must do it

X 5. I do it both well and easily

_____ 6. I do not do it well or easily

_____ 7. I do it well but not easily

_____ 8. I find that time neither flies nor drags when doing it

X 9. I realize that time usually passes quickly while doing it

_____ 10. I am neither exhausted nor energized when I finish

X 11. I am often energized after doing it

_____ 12. I procrastinate doing it

_____ 13. I am neutral about it, neither anticipate nor dread it

X 14. I anticipate it with pleasure

_____ 15. I am usually exhausted when I have finished doing it

Activity #1

_____

_____

_____

_____ 1. I find that time drags by when doing it

_____ 2. I enjoy doing it

_____ 3. I would prefer to delegate or hire it out if possible

_____ 4. I dread doing it but must do it, or believe/ have been taught that I must do it

_____ 5. I do it both well and easily

_____ 6. I do not do it well or easily

_____ 7. I do it well but not easily

_____ 8. I find that time neither flies nor drags when doing it

_____ 9. I realize that time usually passes quickly while doing it

_____ 10. I am neither exhausted nor energized when I finish

_____ 11. I am often energized after doing it

_____ 12. I procrastinate doing it

_____ 13. I am neutral about it, neither anticipate nor dread it

_____ 14. I anticipate it with pleasure

_____ 15. I am usually exhausted when I have finished doing it

Activity #2

_____

_____

_____

_____ 1. I find that time drags by when doing it

_____ 2. I enjoy doing it

_____ 3. I would prefer to delegate or hire it out
if possible

_____ 4. I dread doing it but must do it, or believe/
have been taught that I must do it

_____ 5. I do it both well and easily

_____ 6. I do not do it well or easily

_____ 7. I do it well but not easily

_____ 8. I find that time neither flies nor drags
when doing it

_____ 9. I realize that time usually passes quickly
while doing it

_____ 10. I am neither exhausted nor energized
when I finish

_____ 11. I am often energized after doing it

_____ 12. I procrastinate doing it

_____ 13. I am neutral about it, neither anticipate
nor dread it

_____ 14. I anticipate it with pleasure

_____ 15. I am usually exhausted when I have
finished doing it

Activity #3

_____

_____

_____

_____ 1. I find that time drags by when doing it

_____ 2. I enjoy doing it

_____ 3. I would prefer to delegate or hire it out
if possible

_____ 4. I dread doing it but must do it, or believe/
have been taught that I must do it

_____ 5. I do it both well and easily

_____ 6. I do not do it well or easily

_____ 7. I do it well but not easily

_____ 8. I find that time neither flies nor drags
when doing it

_____ 9. I realize that time usually passes quickly
while doing it

_____ 10. I am neither exhausted nor energized
when I finish

_____ 11. I am often energized after doing it

_____ 12. I procrastinate doing it

_____ 13. I am neutral about it, neither anticipate
nor dread it

_____ 14. I anticipate it with pleasure

_____ 15. I am usually exhausted when I have
finished doing it

Activity #4

_____

_____

_____

____ 1. I find that time drags by when doing it

____ 2. I enjoy doing it

____ 3. I would prefer to delegate or hire it out
        if possible

____ 4. I dread doing it but must do it, or believe/
        have been taught that I must do it

____ 5. I do it both well and easily

____ 6. I do not do it well or easily

____ 7. I do it well but not easily

____ 8. I find that time neither flies nor drags
        when doing it

____ 9. I realize that time usually passes quickly
        while doing it

____ 10. I am neither exhausted nor energized
        when I finish

____ 11. I am often energized after doing it

____ 12. I procrastinate doing it

____ 13. I am neutral about it, neither anticipate
        nor dread it

____ 14. I anticipate it with pleasure

____ 15. I am usually exhausted when I have
        finished doing it

Activity #5

_____

_____

_____

_____ 1. I find that time drags by when doing it

_____ 2. I enjoy doing it

_____ 3. I would prefer to delegate or hire it out
if possible

_____ 4. I dread doing it but must do it, or believe/
have been taught that I must do it

_____ 5. I do it both well and easily

_____ 6. I do not do it well or easily

_____ 7. I do it well but not easily

_____ 8. I find that time neither flies nor drags
when doing it

_____ 9. I realize that time usually passes quickly
while doing it

_____ 10. I am neither exhausted nor energized
when I finish

_____ 11. I am often energized after doing it

_____ 12. I procrastinate doing it

_____ 13. I am neutral about it, neither anticipate
nor dread it

_____ 14. I anticipate it with pleasure

_____ 15. I am usually exhausted when I have
finished doing it

Activity #6

_____

_____

_____

____ 1. I find that time drags by when doing it

____ 2. I enjoy doing it

____ 3. I would prefer to delegate or hire it out
if possible

____ 4. I dread doing it but must do it, or believe/
have been taught that I must do it

____ 5. I do it both well and easily

____ 6. I do not do it well or easily

____ 7. I do it well but not easily

____ 8. I find that time neither flies nor drags
when doing it

____ 9. I realize that time usually passes quickly
while doing it

____ 10. I am neither exhausted nor energized
when I finish

____ 11. I am often energized after doing it

____ 12. I procrastinate doing it

____ 13. I am neutral about it, neither anticipate
nor dread it

____ 14. I anticipate it with pleasure

____ 15. I am usually exhausted when I have
finished doing it

Activity #7

_____

_____

_____

___ 1. I find that time drags by when doing it

___ 2. I enjoy doing it

___ 3. I would prefer to delegate or hire it out
   if possible

___ 4. I dread doing it but must do it, or believe/
   have been taught that I must do it

___ 5. I do it both well and easily

___ 6. I do not do it well or easily

___ 7. I do it well but not easily

___ 8. I find that time neither flies nor drags
   when doing it

___ 9. I realize that time usually passes quickly
   while doing it

___ 10. I am neither exhausted nor energized
   when I finish

___ 11. I am often energized after doing it

___ 12. I procrastinate doing it

___ 13. I am neutral about it, neither anticipate
   nor dread it

___ 14. I anticipate it with pleasure

___ 15. I am usually exhausted when I have
   finished doing it

Activity #8

_____

_____

_____

_____ 1. I find that time drags by when doing it

_____ 2. I enjoy doing it

_____ 3. I would prefer to delegate or hire it out if possible

_____ 4. I dread doing it but must do it, or believe/ have been taught that I must do it

_____ 5. I do it both well and easily

_____ 6. I do not do it well or easily

_____ 7. I do it well but not easily

_____ 8. I find that time neither flies nor drags when doing it

_____ 9. I realize that time usually passes quickly while doing it

_____ 10. I am neither exhausted nor energized when I finish

_____ 11. I am often energized after doing it

_____ 12. I procrastinate doing it

_____ 13. I am neutral about it, neither anticipate nor dread it

_____ 14. I anticipate it with pleasure

_____ 15. I am usually exhausted when I have finished doing it

Activity #9

_____

_____

_____

_____ 1. I find that time drags by when doing it

_____ 2. I enjoy doing it

_____ 3. I would prefer to delegate or hire it out if possible

_____ 4. I dread doing it but must do it, or believe/ have been taught that I must do it

_____ 5. I do it both well and easily

_____ 6. I do not do it well or easily

_____ 7. I do it well but not easily

_____ 8. I find that time neither flies nor drags when doing it

_____ 9. I realize that time usually passes quickly while doing it

_____ 10. I am neither exhausted nor energized when I finish

_____ 11. I am often energized after doing it

_____ 12. I procrastinate doing it

_____ 13. I am neutral about it, neither anticipate nor dread it

_____ 14. I anticipate it with pleasure

_____ 15. I am usually exhausted when I have finished doing it

Activity #10

_____

_____

_____

_____ 1. I find that time drags by when doing it

_____ 2. I enjoy doing it

_____ 3. I would prefer to delegate or hire it out if possible

_____ 4. I dread doing it but must do it, or believe/ have been taught that I must do it

_____ 5. I do it both well and easily

_____ 6. I do not do it well or easily

_____ 7. I do it well but not easily

_____ 8. I find that time neither flies nor drags when doing it

_____ 9. I realize that time usually passes quickly while doing it

_____ 10. I am neither exhausted nor energized when I finish

_____ 11. I am often energized after doing it

_____ 12. I procrastinate doing it

_____ 13. I am neutral about it, neither anticipate nor dread it

_____ 14. I anticipate it with pleasure

_____ 15. I am usually exhausted when I have finished doing it

Activity #11

_____

_____

_____

_____ 1. I find that time drags by when doing it

_____ 2. I enjoy doing it

_____ 3. I would prefer to delegate or hire it out
if possible

_____ 4. I dread doing it but must do it, or believe/
have been taught that I must do it

_____ 5. I do it both well and easily

_____ 6. I do not do it well or easily

_____ 7. I do it well but not easily

_____ 8. I find that time neither flies nor drags
when doing it

_____ 9. I realize that time usually passes quickly
while doing it

_____ 10. I am neither exhausted nor energized
when I finish

_____ 11. I am often energized after doing it

_____ 12. I procrastinate doing it

_____ 13. I am neutral about it, neither anticipate
nor dread it

_____ 14. I anticipate it with pleasure

_____ 15. I am usually exhausted when I have
finished doing it

Activity #12

_____

_____

_____

_____ 1. I find that time drags by when doing it

_____ 2. I enjoy doing it

_____ 3. I would prefer to delegate or hire it out
          if possible

_____ 4. I dread doing it but must do it, or believe/
          have been taught that I must do it

_____ 5. I do it both well and easily

_____ 6. I do not do it well or easily

_____ 7. I do it well but not easily

_____ 8. I find that time neither flies nor drags
          when doing it

_____ 9. I realize that time usually passes quickly
          while doing it

_____ 10. I am neither exhausted nor energized
          when I finish

_____ 11. I am often energized after doing it

_____ 12. I procrastinate doing it

_____ 13. I am neutral about it, neither anticipate
          nor dread it

_____ 14. I anticipate it with pleasure

_____ 15. I am usually exhausted when I have
          finished doing it

Scoring Your Evaluation

Go back to each activity and transfer your marks to the following answer keys. After transfering your 5 marks for all twelve activites, write in the points value for each number you have marked and total the points column in the box provided. An example has been completed for you.

Activity #1 (Example from page 133)
Answer Key

_____	1. = 0 points	_____
X	2. = 5 points	5
_____	3. = 3 points	_____
_____	4. = 0 points	_____
X	5. = 5 points	5
_____	6. = 0 points	_____
_____	7. = 3 points	_____
_____	8. = 3 points	_____
X	9. = 5 points	5
_____	10. = 3 points	_____
X	11. = 5 points	5
_____	12. = 0 points	_____
_____	13. = 3 points	_____
X	14. = 5 points	5
_____	15. = 0 points	_____

Total Points   25

Activity #1
Answer Key

_____ 1. = 0 points _____

_____ 2. = 5 points _____

_____ 3. = 3 points _____

_____ 4. = 0 points _____

_____ 5. = 5 points _____

_____ 6. = 0 points _____

_____ 7. = 3 points _____

_____ 8. = 3 points _____

_____ 9. = 5 points _____

_____ 10. = 3 points _____

_____ 11. = 5 points _____

_____ 12. = 0 points _____

_____ 13. = 3 points _____

_____ 14. = 5 points _____

_____ 15. = 0 points _____

Total Points ☐

Activity #2
Answer Key

_____ 1. = 0 points _____

_____ 2. = 5 points _____

_____ 3. = 3 points _____

_____ 4. = 0 points _____

_____ 5. = 5 points _____

_____ 6. = 0 points _____

_____ 7. = 3 points _____

_____ 8. = 3 points _____

_____ 9. = 5 points _____

_____ 10. = 3 points _____

_____ 11. = 5 points _____

_____ 12. = 0 points _____

_____ 13. = 3 points _____

_____ 14. = 5 points _____

_____ 15. = 0 points _____

Total Points ☐

Activity #3
Answer Key

_____ 1. = 0 points _____
_____ 2. = 5 points _____
_____ 3. = 3 points _____
_____ 4. = 0 points _____
_____ 5. = 5 points _____
_____ 6. = 0 points _____
_____ 7. = 3 points _____
_____ 8. = 3 points _____
_____ 9. = 5 points _____
_____ 10. = 3 points _____
_____ 11. = 5 points _____
_____ 12. = 0 points _____
_____ 13. = 3 points _____
_____ 14. = 5 points _____
_____ 15. = 0 points _____

Total Points

Activity #4
Answer Key

_____ 1. = 0 points _____
_____ 2. = 5 points _____
_____ 3. = 3 points _____
_____ 4. = 0 points _____
_____ 5. = 5 points _____
_____ 6. = 0 points _____
_____ 7. = 3 points _____
_____ 8. = 3 points _____
_____ 9. = 5 points _____
_____ 10. = 3 points _____
_____ 11. = 5 points _____
_____ 12. = 0 points _____
_____ 13. = 3 points _____
_____ 14. = 5 points _____
_____ 15. = 0 points _____

Total Points

Activity #5
Answer Key

_____ 1. = 0 points _____
_____ 2. = 5 points _____
_____ 3. = 3 points _____
_____ 4. = 0 points _____
_____ 5. = 5 points _____
_____ 6. = 0 points _____
_____ 7. = 3 points _____
_____ 8. = 3 points _____
_____ 9. = 5 points _____
_____ 10. = 3 points _____
_____ 11. = 5 points _____
_____ 12. = 0 points _____
_____ 13. = 3 points _____
_____ 14. = 5 points _____
_____ 15. = 0 points _____

Total Points ☐

Activity #6
Answer Key

_____ 1. = 0 points _____
_____ 2. = 5 points _____
_____ 3. = 3 points _____
_____ 4. = 0 points _____
_____ 5. = 5 points _____
_____ 6. = 0 points _____
_____ 7. = 3 points _____
_____ 8. = 3 points _____
_____ 9. = 5 points _____
_____ 10. = 3 points _____
_____ 11. = 5 points _____
_____ 12. = 0 points _____
_____ 13. = 3 points _____
_____ 14. = 5 points _____
_____ 15. = 0 points _____

Total Points ☐

Activity #7
Answer Key

_____ 1. = 0 points _____
_____ 2. = 5 points _____
_____ 3. = 3 points _____
_____ 4. = 0 points _____
_____ 5. = 5 points _____
_____ 6. = 0 points _____
_____ 7. = 3 points _____
_____ 8. = 3 points _____
_____ 9. = 5 points _____
_____ 10. = 3 points _____
_____ 11. = 5 points _____
_____ 12. = 0 points _____
_____ 13. = 3 points _____
_____ 14. = 5 points _____
_____ 15. = 0 points _____

Total Points

Activity #8
Answer Key

_____ 1. = 0 points _____
_____ 2. = 5 points _____
_____ 3. = 3 points _____
_____ 4. = 0 points _____
_____ 5. = 5 points _____
_____ 6. = 0 points _____
_____ 7. = 3 points _____
_____ 8. = 3 points _____
_____ 9. = 5 points _____
_____ 10. = 3 points _____
_____ 11. = 5 points _____
_____ 12. = 0 points _____
_____ 13. = 3 points _____
_____ 14. = 5 points _____
_____ 15. = 0 points _____

Total Points

Activity #9
Answer Key

_____ 1. = 0 points _____
_____ 2. = 5 points _____
_____ 3. = 3 points _____
_____ 4. = 0 points _____
_____ 5. = 5 points _____
_____ 6. = 0 points _____
_____ 7. = 3 points _____
_____ 8. = 3 points _____
_____ 9. = 5 points _____
_____ 10. = 3 points _____
_____ 11. = 5 points _____
_____ 12. = 0 points _____
_____ 13. = 3 points _____
_____ 14. = 5 points _____
_____ 15. = 0 points _____

Total Points [ ]

Activity #10
Answer Key

_____ 1. = 0 points _____
_____ 2. = 5 points _____
_____ 3. = 3 points _____
_____ 4. = 0 points _____
_____ 5. = 5 points _____
_____ 6. = 0 points _____
_____ 7. = 3 points _____
_____ 8. = 3 points _____
_____ 9. = 5 points _____
_____ 10. = 3 points _____
_____ 11. = 5 points _____
_____ 12. = 0 points _____
_____ 13. = 3 points _____
_____ 14. = 5 points _____
_____ 15. = 0 points _____

Total Points [ ]

Activity #11
Answer Key

_____ 1. = 0 points _____
_____ 2. = 5 points _____
_____ 3. = 3 points _____
_____ 4. = 0 points _____
_____ 5. = 5 points _____
_____ 6. = 0 points _____
_____ 7. = 3 points _____
_____ 8. = 3 points _____
_____ 9. = 5 points _____
_____ 10. = 3 points _____
_____ 11. = 5 points _____
_____ 12. = 0 points _____
_____ 13. = 3 points _____
_____ 14. = 5 points _____
_____ 15. = 0 points _____

Total Points

Activity #12
Answer Key

_____ 1. = 0 points _____
_____ 2. = 5 points _____
_____ 3. = 3 points _____
_____ 4. = 0 points _____
_____ 5. = 5 points _____
_____ 6. = 0 points _____
_____ 7. = 3 points _____
_____ 8. = 3 points _____
_____ 9. = 5 points _____
_____ 10. = 3 points _____
_____ 11. = 5 points _____
_____ 12. = 0 points _____
_____ 13. = 3 points _____
_____ 14. = 5 points _____
_____ 15. = 0 points _____

Total Points

A score of 16 or above

This indicates that the activity is likely a good match for your brain bent. That doesn't mean that 100% of the activity matches your brain bent, but at least 51% does!

A score between 9 and 15

This implies that this activity is a borderline match. If it is an activity that must be done, compensate for the increased energy drain by spending some time before or after doing something that is easier for your brain.

A score of 9 or below

This suggests that this activity may be a poor match for your brain. If you believed you had the option and there were no negative consequences, you might choose to never do this activity again, do it very infrequently, or hire it out.

A Higher Score Means a Better Match

Remember, the higher your score the more likely it is that the activity is a good match with your brain bent. The lower the score, the less likely the activity matches your brain bent and the more fatigue you may experience. This assumes that your lifestyle is sufficiently in balance, that you have energy, and aren't approaching everything from a position of fatigue.

The preferred pattern is one where the majority of activities are those that your brain does easily. If your brain anticipates the task or activity with pleasure, accomplishing it will likely not put as large a dent in your brain's energy bank. To thrive, strive for a 51% match overall between your activities in life and your own brain bent.

If a nonpreferred pattern emerges—a pattern of activities that your brain dreads and procrastinates, a pattern of activities you do well but not easily and that can make a huge dent in your energy bank—you may want to develop a plan that will allow you to reduce the time spent performing activities that are energy intensive.

By the time you apply this set of statements to a few activities, you'll probably be able to estimate in your head. That's a helpful skill to hone, especially when you are asked if you're willing to help with a specific task. Knowing up front whether a specific activity is likely to be a good match with your brain bent is a real deal!

Bent and Best

What type of brain bent results in the best teacher, minister, doctor, engineer, chef, sales person, secretary, waitress, or whatever? The answer is pretty straightforward. All things being equal, the difference will lie in how easily the brain can accomplish the required tasks.

Almost anyone can select a career and then learn the tasks required. The best at a specific career will likely be the individual who has a bent that matches the required key tasks.

When trying to decide what type of work to pursue, questions you might want to ask yourself include:

- How much energy will it take me to learn the skills?

- Can I do the required tasks well and easily, or well but not easily?

- On a daily basis, how much energy will it take me to accomplish the tasks associated with that job or career?

- How much energy will I have left for my personal life?

It's all about using your brain's energy efficiently! Keep in mind that individuals with differing brain bents may select a similar career, but will approach that career from varying perspectives. They may also achieve differing degrees of competence, and more or less overall success, based on what their brains do easily.

A Good Match

Is it possible to match 100% of your life's activities with what your brain does easily and energy-efficiently? Probably not. It might not even be desirable, because you do have a whole brain, and you need to be able to use all portions of it—at least some of the time. A desirable goal is to match a majority of your life's activities with your brain bent. That, it would appear, is at least 51%.

The more skilled you become at evaluating what your own brain does easily, the more quickly you can make decisions that can benefit you in positive ways. It may mean that you start searching for a job that will give you a better match. It may mean that because you have put a great deal of time and energy into learning your present job, even though it's only a 40% match, you choose to stay in that job and engage in a higher percentage of activities that are energy-efficient for your brain during off hours.

Easily Versus Well

Growing up, many of us were told that if something wasn't difficult to accomplish, it probably wasn't worth doing. Based on emerging brain-function studies, the opposite appears to be true. The easier a task is for your brain to accomplish, the more it feels like "playing," the more likely it is to be a match with your own innate preferences.

And then there is the old saying, "If at first you don't succeed, try, try again." If at first you don't succeed, maybe you should try again. Practice tends to make perfect (or at least better). Eventually you may want to evaluate how much energy you are expending and decide if it is worth it to you. Sometimes it is. Remember that it took Steve Fossett several tries to fly around the world in a balloon. On the other hand, you may decide it isn't worth it to you, and you should move on to something that is a better match with your innate giftedness, and that requires less expenditure of energy. The bottom line: there is a huge difference between what one has learned to do well and what one's brain does easily!

Literary Link...

> *You've got to take your brain out of your head every once in a while and jump on it.*
> —Mark Twain

Moving Toward Success

Why does matching a majority of your life's activities with your brain bent increase your likelihood of success? Here are a few reasons:

- Your brain is usually able to help you develop higher levels of competence in areas of preference. Increased competence often contributes to increased success.

- Your brain tends to expend less energy when engaged in activities that match its bent. Being able to accomplish activities easily and energy-efficiently can contribute to your success, especially over the long haul. Your energy may last longer because you're withdrawing it from your energy bank in smaller increments.

- The better match you have between your abilities and your brain bent, the more likely you are to be healthy and achieve your longevity potential. When you aren't able to achieve a match between the majority of your activities and your brain bent, the risk goes up for experiencing health problems, discouragement, fatigue, and shortened life.

- The brain and immune system are in constant communication. One way to strengthen the immune system is to keep your brain happy. In general, a happy brain makes for a happy body.

Examples abound of individuals who identified their own brain bent and took advantage of it. George Burns, for instance, wanted to make people laugh and found a way to do it as a career. That's probably one reason he lived to the century mark (or close to it) and was performing on stage almost until the day of his death. And what about Lucille Ball and Michael Jordan, Oprah Winfrey and Paul McCartney, Bill Gates and Johnny Cash, Steven Spielberg and Candace Pert, and on and on? These are individuals who obviously managed to match the majority of their activities to their own brain's innate advantage. In fact, that may be one of the keys to what our culture defines as mega-success. A good match!

Neil's Story

In 1989, Robin Williams starred in the wonderful true story of a college professor named John Keating. The book and movie, "Dead Poet's Society", touched the hearts of many teachers and parents. There was one especially memorable and sensitive scene where student Neil Perry was chosen to play the part of Puck (a leading role) in the school's production of Shakespeare's "Midsummer Night's Dream." However, Neil's father, a no-nonsense authoritarian, wanted Neil to become a doctor and forbade him to be in the play. Neil went to talk to Mr. Keating. The boy's dilemma was whether to conform to his father's wishes or follow his heart's longing. The dialogue went something like this:

> Taking a deep breath Neil said: "My father is making me quit the play... Acting is everything to me, Mr. Keating. It's what I want to do!"

"Have you told your father what you just told me? About your passion for acting?" Mr. Keating asked.

"Are you kidding? He'd kill me!"

"Talk to him, Neil," Keating urged.

"Isn't there an easier way?" Neil begged.

"Not if you're going to stay true to yourself."

Ah, staying true to yourself. That's not so easy. It can be very challenging for so-called adults—and even more difficult for those whose brains are not yet mature. However, staying true to yourself can set you free to live your own innate giftedness. It involves determining your brain bent and pursuing what you love to do—what your brain does easily. Sure, you can choose to ignore your innate giftedness, but only to the detriment of your happiness, wellness, and perhaps even longevity.

It's not always easy, however. There's a price to be paid for living your own innate giftedness. But, that price can come with a remarkable return on the investment.

Simple but Not Always Easy

To reiterate, the concept is simple, but implementation is not always easy. It can take hard work to stay true to yourself in the midst of your relationship system. This is illustrated in Neil's story. The results can be deadly if you do not know how to be true to yourself and stay meaningfully connected to significant others. Neil's father resisted his son's desires. That's not unusual. Many people resist at some time or another, especially when they believe theirs is the best course to take, or the preferred choice, or the right way, or they are in charge (e.g., parent, teacher, care giver). Resistance can pop up in a heartbeat.

Earlier we mentioned examples of individuals who identified their own brain bent and took advantage of it. And yet, when you consider their family systems, there is this undercurrent of struggle. Other individuals offered hope that gave the strugglers courage to succeed.

Changes can disrupt the stability of your relationships, at least temporarily. Whenever one person in a system wants to change, any degree of change will impact the others who are emotionally close. And why should they not be resistant to change that they did not initiate or even think about? That is human nature. Just because you make changes does not mean others will accept the changes or go along with them. This resistance in the relationship system can consume more energy than you will gain, unless you know and plan for the changes in yourself and for the reaction in your relationship system.

Having the courage to be yourself always leads you back to the management of yourself within the context of your important relationships. This is how you build an emotional backbone for becoming a more autonomous and joyful self. It may be a divorce, death, disease, new baby, job, marriage, or one of many other events that triggers the impulse or desire to take a stand for self. To be successful it will be important to develop the necessary emotional maturity to define yourself in difficult relationships.

Your Own Drummer

Henry Wriston wrote: "A guidance counselor who has made a fetish of security, or who has unwittingly surrendered his thinking to economic determinism, may steer a youth away from his dream of becoming a poet, an artist, a musician, or any other of thousands of things because it offers no security, it does not pay well, there are no vacancies, it has no future. Among all the tragic consequences of depression and war, this suppression of personal self-expression through one's life work is among the most poignant."

Learning to live authentically, to match the majority of your life's activities to what your brain does easily, might be compared to "marching to the beat of your own drummer." As the Bible puts it, this is knowing "the way [you] should go"—Proverbs 22:6. And yes, the truth—about who you are innately—can set you free to live authentically, to thrive, and to be the person you were designed to be.

Literary Link...

A window in Merton's mind let in that strange light of surprise in which we see for the first time things we have known all along.

—Gilbert Keith Chesterton in "The Three Tools of Death"

If you are just learning about thinking brain bent for the first time, it may be a lightbulb experience. Hang in there. Find your true path. It's where your brain knew you belonged all along! When you know who you are and match the majority of your activities to your innate giftedness, you'll usually have more energy and better mental, physical, and spiritual health.

We always give up something to get something. There is a price to be paid for everything. A price for following your own drummer. It may even require great amounts of courage and large expenditures of energy, initially, but the rewards can be tremendous in the long term.

There's a price to be paid for not following your own drummer. A price of diminished rewards.

CHAPTER SIX
Up the Down Escalator

Ignoring who you truly, authentically are can literally be killing you... Forcing yourself to be someone you are not, or stuffing down who you really are, is incredibly taxing. It will tax you so much that it will shorten your life by years and years.

— Philip C. McGraw, in Self Matters

A familiar slogan goes "Do it anyway. It builds character." Is this saying part of the great American myth, or just something Grandpa said? Either way, current brain research doesn't appear to agree with this axiom.

Doing things you don't like to do and doing them often doesn't necessarily build character. It more likely creates bitterness or frustration or, as we've been saying, brain drain! However, people who have absorbed such beliefs and expectations often struggle their entire lives trying to develop skills in areas that are exceedingly difficult, if not downright exhausting. It's a bit like trying to ascend an escalator that is on its way down. Not your best choice if you want to live a long life that's healthy, happy, and successful!

Competencies

Competencies are simply skills that have been honed through practice. You can develop competencies in areas of innate preference as well as non-preference. When the skills you develop match your innate preference, you're usually able to achieve higher levels of competency, meaning you're better at performing those skills than others.

For example, if you put a pen or pencil in your favored writing hand and sign your name, you'll be exercising a developed competency in an area of preference. Now put the pen in your non-favored hand and try signing your name. Observe differences in ease of writing and legibility, and pay close attention to the amount of energy you expend in the second exercise. Without even doing that right now, you can probably remember the stress from attempting it at some time in the past. When you write with your non-preferred hand, the activity will generally require a higher expenditure of energy and result in a lower level of comfort, even if you improve your writing in that hand through practice.

Here's another example. Fold your hands, fingers interlocking, in your preferred style. We do this so automatically that you probably followed this direction without giving much thought to it. Look at your folded hands. Which thumb is on top, right or left? How comfortable do your hands feel? Refold your hands, interlocking your fingers so that the opposite thumb is on top. How comfortable do your hands feel in this position?

This exercise demonstrates the phenomenon known as adaption. We can fold our hands the opposite way and, with practice, this style will become less awkward. But it's unlikely that it will ever feel as comfortable as our preferred folding style.

A similar thing happens inside our brain when we utilize non-preferred functions. We just can't observe it as easily as we can with the hand-folding exercise.

Literary Link...

The surest way to live with honor in the world is to be in reality what we would appear to be.

—Socrates

Building Competencies

You may have deliberately chosen to develop skills throughout your thinking brain, even as you deliberately strive for a majority match between your activities and your brain preferences. Or you may decide you need to do so. If that's the case, here are some examples of competency-building activities, separated according to the four divisions of the thinking brain (although there may be some overlap).

Left Frontal Lobe

- Join a debate club
- Give a speech in public
- Read information and write a summary/abstract
- Participate in a research project

Right Frontal Lobe

- Write poems and stories
- Learn to meditate
- Compose and/or arrange music
- Draw, paint, sculpt, carve, design, assemble 3-D puzzles, travel

Left Posterior Lobes

- Read and outline the information
- Make and follow lists
- Balance the checkbook
- Join a club or team
- Learn to sight-read music

Right Posterior Lobes

- Join a choir or other singing group
- Take a drama class
- Play games for fun
- Participate in peer counseling
- Play an instrument by ear

What Is Adaption?

The concept of adaption relates to an ability to change in order to be able to fit into a new or specified situation. In brain-function terminology, it refers to the development and use of competencies or skills that do not match one's areas of preference—one's areas of innate giftedness. The concept of adaption can apply to any area of brain function (e.g., spending large amounts of time functioning at a non-preferred position on the Gender Continuum or the EAI Continuum, or repressing our preferred sensory system, or failing to utilize our brain bent).

All human beings adapt, and it's a good thing! How pathetically limited life would be if people functioned only from a position of innate preference. An individual whose brain bent favors the right frontal lobe may be quite entrepreneurial or artistically creative (e.g., painting, drawing, writing poetry/stories, composing music). However, this same individual also might want the option to be able to balance a checkbook (left posterior lobes), connect with friends and family (right posterior lobes), and analyze key reports and make decisions about financial investments (left frontal lobe). Those can represent helpful and necessary adaptions.

Adaption actually increases our options. That's the up side. Remember: there is a huge difference between what you have learned to do well and what your brain does easily. Your overall potential for success increases when you have developed skills throughout your brain. The difference is the amount of time you spend engaged in activities that are preferred versus non-preferred. If you are spending the majority of your time performing activities that are non-preferred, it can be completely exhausting. That's the down side.

Mel Levine put it like this, "Nothing is as stressful as trying to be a different person from who you are."

Sarah's Story
Sarah sat slumped in the chair, head in her hands. "I'm so exhausted that I can't put one foot in front of the other!" Sarah had worked in the family-owned business for eighteen years. The detail that was required to offer a reliable service to customers drained her energy. Not only was she perpetually tired, some rather serious health problems had cropped up.

The doctor suggested that Sarah apply the

energy-evaluation process (see Chapter Five) to her activities both at home and at work. She was amazed at what she uncovered! Together they worked out a plan of action, beginning with a schedule of after-work activities that were easy for Sarah's brain. Often, by the end of the activity (e.g., art class at the local Junior College, singing with the community choir), Sarah reported she had more energy than when she had started. She was sleeping better, too.

With some measure of trepidation (a few family members were quite verbal about Sarah's need to avoid being selfish and lazy), she hired a part-time housekeeper. This freed up time to engage in activities that she enjoyed and decreased some of the energy drain.

Different Strokes...

Adaption represents the quintessential "different strokes for different folks" philosophy. A task that constitutes adaption in one person can represent giftedness in another. An activity that energizes one person can exhaust another. A task that one individual can ace at high levels of competence may be virtually impossible for another to accomplish at that level, if at all. Why? Because one's innate giftedness matches the needs of the task better.

Thus, the same activity can either be desirable or undesirable based on the amount of brain energy required, the amount of time devoted to the activity, and the individual's own innate giftedness. For some individuals, learning to balance the checkbook and doing it every month could represent desirable adaption. Becoming an accountant, bookkeeper, or CPA might be undesirable. For others, offering a listening ear for a few hours a month as a peer counselor might fall into the category of desirable adaption. Working full time as a counselor might represent undesirable adaption and lead to burnout. Writing a short article for the newspaper might help to build desirable skills. Expecting to earn one's living as a writer might be an entirely different matter. And so on. The key to success is to adapt for short periods of time (temporary adaption) rather than for long periods of time (prolonged adaption).

Adaption Costs

As beneficial as temporary adaption can be, there is a cost. Human beings pay for it in some way or another—mostly in life energy. Benziger, creator of the Benziger Thinking Styles Assessment that includes information on one's risk for adaption, summarizes the cost of adaption as follows:

- The immediate results tend to be that second for second the brain works much harder (e.g., increased need for oxygen, glucose, and other nutrients)

- The short-term results tend to be an increase in irritability, headaches, and difficulty in mastering new tasks

- The long-term results tend to include exhaustion, depression, lack of joy, a homeostatic imbalance involving oxygen and glucose, premature aging of the brain, and a vulnerability to illness

Triggers for Prolonged Adaption

People adapt for a variety of reasons. Examples of situations that can push one toward prolonged adaption include:

- A mismatch between your brain bent and societal expectations for your gender (e.g., a female who is gifted in auto mechanics or research, a male who is gifted in home decorating or cooking)

- A mismatch between your innate giftedness and guidelines for behaviors (e.g., your religion discourages dancing or acting; a teacher demeans musical or artistic talent, your parents insist on your pursuing a specific career)

- Your position in the sibling lineup (e.g., an oldest or only son is expected to take over the family farm or family-owned company regardless of personal desire or aptitude)

- Being rewarded for adaptive behaviors or shamed for one's innate giftedness (e.g., "You're smart enough to be a doctor. Forget teaching!" "No son of mine is going to be an artist!" "We'll all be so proud of you if you choose nursing as a career!" "We want you to be an accountant, or nurse, or you-name-it, just like members of this family have always done.")

- Living in an environment that involves mental, emotional, sexual, physical, or spiritual abuse (e.g., you cope by becoming involved in an addictive behavior, you conform to expectations regardless of how much energy it requires)

- Demands of a crisis situation or a lack of opportunity for activities that match your innate giftedness (e.g., you are gifted in creative writing but have no time to spend on it, since you have been left to care for the family; you have musical talent but there is no money for lessons or instruments; your choice of a profession is put down or not encouraged, or the education is unavailable in your area)

- Mimicking a loved family member or disowning characteristics of a disliked member (e.g., your professor-father abandons the family and, although you sense a calling to be a teacher, you don't want to be like him; your favorite aunt is a nurse and you want to be just like her, even though many of her nursing activities are energy intensive for your brain)

- A search for personal identity (e.g., you attempt to differentiate from your twin; you try to excel in activities that are rewarded in your family, even though they don't match your innate preferences; you attempt to succeed by excelling in something that is different from what other family members do; you try to live up to the reputation set by an older sibling)

Living Authentically

Being real and living authentically involves knowing your innate preferences (your brain's advantage and what it does most easily), and making conscious choices related to the type of adaption you exhibit and the amount of time you spend adapting.

Ask yourself: Have I ever lived authentically? Today, do the majority of my activities in life match my innate preferences?

If your answers are yes, you know what it feels like to be real. You likely know how to manage your energy expenditure efficiently. If the answers are no, this may be new territory for you!

Tom's Story

From the time he was a little boy visiting his uncle's ranch, Tom had been fascinated by big machines. No surprise that he became a heavy equipment operator. Reluctantly, due to family pressure, he returned to school. Upon graduation he took over managing the books in his father's prestigious law office. As time went by, however, Tom's health began to deteriorate and signs of depression surfaced. Medication helped but didn't cure his fatigue, boredom, or depression. His uncle, concerned about his favorite nephew, invited Tom to spend a couple of weeks on the ranch. By the time he returned home, Tom had decided to resign his job with the law firm and return to his first love, operating heavy equipment.

His wife tells the story this way: "When Tom bounded up the steps with energy he hadn't shown for years, I knew I had my husband back!"

Managing Adaption

Why is it important to identify and resolve prolonged adaption? The short answer is: because the cost of prolonged adaption is high. It involves expending life energy that is, consequently, unavailable for other endeavors.

The long answer is more involved. Over time, prolonged adaption, with its increased drain on vital energy, can lead to a variety of challenges. These can include:

> Procrastination
> Fatigue
> Risk of illness
> Frustration
> Risk of burnout
> Risk of midlife crisis
>
> Self-esteem levels
> Emotional tone
> Concentration
> Competency
> Thriving in life
> Success overall

Stress of Prolonged Adaption

Think of adaption as a form of stress—a major stressor when it's excessive or prolonged. If you spend years living at high levels of adaption, living an inauthentic life, the stress can eventually show itself in a variety of ways. These can include:

Fatigue: This makes sense, especially when the brain must work significantly harder in adaption situations. The risk here is self-medicating through addictive behaviors such as taking drugs or alcohol, sex, gambling, or anything that will alter brain chemicals and make the person feel better, however temporarily.

Hypervigilance: This becomes sort of a safety mechanism for the brain. It goes on "protective alertness" in response to the mismatch between who it is and the tasks it is being required to complete.

Immune System Suppression: Over time this can show itself in slowed rates of healing and increased susceptibility to illness (e.g., colds or flu, autoimmune diseases, cancer). The brain and immune system are in constant communication. According to Dr. Paris Kidd, a biomedical nutritionist, if people took proper care of their immune system, the average life span could reach over 100 years—at high levels of mental and physical functioning.

Interference with Frontal Lobe Functions: The stress of adaption can alter neurochemicals throughout the brain and it can be especially unhelpful when it occurs in the frontal lobes (the executive portions). This may be reflected in a decrease in artistic and creative endeavors, a reduced ability to brainstorm options, interference with the ability to make logical/rational decisions, and slowed speed of thinking. When you say, "I just can't think," you're probably right on the money. Something isn't working optimally in the brain!

Note: An alteration in brain chemistry may also impact one's management of willpower, the development and use of conscience, and one's behavioral choices. This is an attention-getting concept, especially when some behaviors can impact the next generation. Some researchers even suggest that human beings may be unable to access free will or be truly intimate with another—intellectual, emotional, physical, sexual, or spiritual—unless they are being authentically real.

Memory Problems: Cortisol, released under stress, can interfere with the function of memory in a variety of ways. For more information on this topic, refer to the book by Dr. Robert Sapolsky of Stanford University, *Why Zebras Don't Get Ulcers*.

Discouragement/Depression: Some estimates indicate that 20 million people in the United States are depressed at any given time, with 15% of those being suicidal. Prolonged adaption likely contributes to this depression.

Self-Esteem Problems: This isn't hard to imagine! You don't feel successful in life, you have many of the other symptoms just listed, and you feel "trapped." No wonder you start questioning your self-worth. A diary called, "Goodbye to Berlin", by Christopher Isherwood, opens this way: "I am a camera with its shutter open, quite passive, recording, not thinking." What a blank, tiring way to go through life!

Neuronal Impact

Studies suggest, and it's worth repeating, that chronic stress from a failure to live authentically can shorten your potential longevity by a decade or more. Not a good choice in most people's books! Notice that some of the ways in which the stress of adaption can eventually show itself (outlined above) are similar to a list of factors (below) that can adversely impact neurons over time:

- Chronic disease (especially heart disease)

- Unresolved grief over personal loss

- Alcohol (immoderate use)

- A sedentary lifestyle

- Lack of stimulation

- A low educational level and an absence of curiosity or a desire to learn

- Malnutrition

- Some drugs / medications

- Depression

Aging and Adaption

Avoiding and/or resolving prolonged adaption can help us go lightly into old age. This means that in and of itself, aging (in the absence of excessive or prolonged adaption) does not need to have a large impact on deterioration of brain function. Many individuals have found their path, followed their preferences, and continued to make valuable contributions to our world as senior citizens. Think of these:

- Franz Joseph Haydn wrote the *Creation* at age 67

- Richard Wagner composed the opera *Parsifal* at age 69

- Actress Katherine Hepburn was still acting in movie roles in her 70s

- Merce Cunningham was still dancing in his 70s

- Grandma Moses started a new career in painting in her 70s

- Giuseppi Verdi wrote the opera *Falstaff* when he was age 80

- Arthur Fiedler was conducting music until his death at age 88

- Martha Graham was still choregraphing in her 90s

- Photographer Imogen Cunningham was still taking pictures in her 90s

That's good news. Actually, that's great news! Even better, we can follow suite!

Leaving a Legacy -The Bigger Picture!

One gift that adults can pass along to the next generation is to role model functionality. In fact, it may be the greatest gift that one can bequeath, since children tend to copy what is role modeled to them. Stories abound of elderly individuals who have said, "If I only had it to do over again...." Or, "If only I could go back for just one day and undo that mistake." Unfortunately, no one can do it over again. Fortunately, it is possible to learn from the mistakes of others and from emerging research. Prevention beats attempts at cure every time!

Steven's Story

Steven Spielberg's mother encouraged, even catered, to her son's passion for filmmaking. Once she intentionally cooked a gallon of cherries jubilee, so the story goes, until it exploded in a pressure cooker. Steve wanted to film the gooey mess in the kitchen. "We never had a chance to say no. Steven didn't understand that word!"

Children need to learn that the English language contains a powerful two-letter word, "No"! But Spielberg's mother obviously made judicious decisions about when to use that word and when not to. If she had not encouraged Steven to follow his own bent, even helped him to do so, we might not have *E.T.* or *Schindler's List*.

Finding your way through life can literally—and metaphorically—be a challenge, even a mess! That's okay. If you're open to it, you can learn more from your mistakes than you ever can from your successes. You can learn from the mistakes of others, too. Eleanor Roosevelt encouraged people to do this, saying, "You can't live long enough to make all of them yourself!"

Literary Link...

Creative energy not allowed to develop will express itself in power gone bad. Creative power gone bad is evil.

—Sam Gilliam, addressing 4MAT Renewal Conference, 1996

Morrie's Story

Is there anyone in America who hasn't read the book *Tuesdays with Morrie*? It was on the national bestseller list for years. Journalist Mitch Albom spent Tuesdays with his former professor Morrie Schwartz—to listen and learn. As Morrie lay dying of Lou Gehrig's disease, he mentored his young friend (and the rest of the world) with wisdom about life, love, and death. And dancing!

On the eleventh Tuesday, the topic was "our culture." The aged professor is speaking:

"Look, no matter where you live, the biggest defect we human beings have is our shortsightedness. We don't see what we could be. We should be looking at our potential, stretching ourselves into everything we can become."

Morrie had it right: One good reason to avoid

prolonged adaption is to set a stellar example for others to follow, both young and old.

A Step at a Time

If you tap into the courage needed to actually be who you were meant to be, that could very well be the spark that empowers others to do the same. Do it one step at a time. But do it. Each experience will build on the previous one. Mark Twain said it this way, "A person who has had a bull by the tail once has learned 60 or 70 times as much as a person who hasn't." That's the value of experience.

Of course it will take some practice, especially if you've played games for a long time, living for years in prolonged adaption. But there are ways to manage adaption and start your journey towards thriving. Here are four to consider:

Mentoring: Find a mentor to help you develop needed skills in areas outside your innate preferences.

Collaborating: Collaborate with others who have different innate preferences. Listen and learn from their giftedness.

Sandwiching: Insert non-preferred activities between those that your brain relates to easily. Alternate the tasks you like to do with those that are less enjoyable and more draining.

Trading: Trade with others—each contributing what his/her brain prefers to do. You cut her hair, she balances your checkbook. You write part of his report, he writes part of yours. The potential is limitless.

Randy's Story

When Randy was eighteen and one week away from high school graduation, a prominent physician and friend of the family invited the boy to lunch. During the conversation, the doctor made an astounding offer.

"Randy," the doctor said, "I want to offer you a deal. I've been an orthopedic surgeon in this town for over thirty years. And I've built up a big practice. None of my three older children were interested in pursuing medicine, and my youngest isn't interested either.

"I'll pay your way through medical school to become a surgeon, if you'll just join my office, and take over my practice when I retire."

Whew! Randy stopped home after the lunch appointment and told his family the story. Then he just sort of laughed, shrugged his shoulders, and left the room.

"Wait, Randy! What did you say?" His mother ran after him, desperate. "You may be turning down the opportunity to earn a hundred thousand dollars a year! Let's not be too hasty here!"

"Mom," he retorted patiently. "You know I'm not cut out to be a doctor. I don't feel the least called into medicine. I don't like blood. Not even a little bit!"

His mother could only whisper. "Well, then, tell him about your sister. She loves blood...."

At the time, his mother thought Randy was a

little bit nuts. In retrospect, she quickly figured out that while he could have made it through medical school (blood or not!), he would have been absolutely miserable. To say nothing of completely exhausted!

Somehow, Randy's brain was telling him what was right for his future—and he listened.

The Price
There is a price to pay for prolonged adaption. It differs for different individuals. Resolving prolonged adaption can result in a positive impact on your health, your happiness, your energy, your relationships, your career, and your overall success in life.

If you've never lived your innate giftedness, it'll be a new and interesting journey. If you have, but got caught in the trap of prolonged adaption, it's time to return home. Your brain can hardly wait!

CHAPTER SEVEN
Following Your Path
(The Journey Continues)

If you begin to understand what you are without trying to change it, then what you are undergoes a transformation.
— J. Krishnamurti

Anne's Story

Anne's eyes fluttered open and focused uncertainly on her surroundings. Where was she? The sight and sounds of the hospital room quickly oriented her. "I'm so exhausted," Anne thought to herself. "I don't have the energy to face this." How had she gotten into this predicament? Hospitalized again!

Adaption. The word popped into her mind. It had started a very long time ago. "At birth," she mused. Anne had spent half a lifetime trying fervently, even desperately, to juggle and satisfy the myriad expectations of family, school, church, friends, society, and work. For the past decade she had managed a large department. Her duties included writing grants, arguing budget allocations, and overseeing dozens of programs, scores of employees, and millions of dollars. She enjoyed very little of it, but to all outward appearances she was very successful. She'd tried her very best to conform to the strong work ethic that had been passed down to her: be a nice girl, follow the rules, and work hard. Everything will come up roses in the end.

But they had been wrong—oh so wrong! Instead of roses, life was flat-out exhausting. Anne usually arrived home to collapse in bed, sleep fitfully for a few hours, and then get up to do it all over again. Periodically she'd crash. Sometimes those crashes were accompanied by illness. Her bouts with pneumonia were one example.

"If I live through this," Anne said aloud to no one in particular, "I'm going to learn everything I can about my brain, and get serious about crafting a life that works for me!"

Fast-forward 20 years. Anne survived and continues on the personal journey that began when her life nearly ended. She stopped adapting excessively, gradually quit fitting into everyone else's model for her life, and sought the path she should have been on in the first place. The results? More energy. Better health. Sheer joy.

When others around her ask Anne, "What's your secret?" her immediate response is, "Know who you are and live it. It's the only way to fly!" And fly she does.

A Quick Review

In Chapter One, we stressed the need to know ourselves, to understand the advantages that have been built into our brains. We can potentially be more successful by living our innate giftedness on a daily basis.

Then we examined some important brain differences between the genders, although as members of the same species, we're more alike than different. Being true to one's own gender—yet understanding the other—is key for collaboration, improved mental health, and peaceful social coexistence.

In Chapter Three, we reviewed extroversion, ambiversion, and introversion, and noted that our brain is wired from birth for its innate position on the EAI Continuum. This position reflects the relative amounts of stimuli our brain craves or can handle before it seeks relief.

Next, the sensory systems were introduced. Most brains have a unique sensory package that amounts to yet another personal preference. Unimpaired, our brains can process visual, auditory, and kinesthetic data, and we do this much of the time. However, one type of stimuli registers in our brain most quickly and impacts not only the way we learn, but also our relationships.

In Chapter Five, we identified that the brain has a bent—a natural preference or advantage that impacts the way you processes information. Understanding your own brain bent and matching the majority of your activities to what your brain does easily, can change your life—positively! It can add life to your years. It might even lengthen it. While the concept is simple, it's not always easy as we attempt to live our innate giftedness against the backdrop of myriad expectations— from self, family, school, career, church, and society; but it's worth the work!

Chapter Six addressed adaption, its definition and its uses. It provided examples of desirable versus undesirable adaption. Temporary adaption is useful and desirable. But for our mental and physical well being, prolonged adaption is not our best option. Again, the concept is simple, but the ongoing application of the information can be a challenge.

Are You Living Authentically?

In this last chapter, we tie this information together and ask you to give an honest answer to the question, "Are you living authentically?" In far too many cases, the answer to that question is, "No". Many individuals have not achieved a desirable match between their innate preferences and their life activities — such as career endeavors, relationship roles, and free time experiences.

Literary Link...

> *To thine own self be true, and it must follow as the night the day, thou canst not then be false to anyone.*
> — Shakespeare in Hamlet

Is this a new problem? Evidently not. Over the centuries writers have spoken to the need to be true to ourselves. The famous lines from Hamlet are just one example and may have been more profound than even Shakespeare realized. Then again, maybe he did. In our fast-paced and often frenetic world, these words may be truer today!

Perhaps the most important factor in living a successful life by design is learning as much as possible about how your brain functions. It is our identity. We cannot do without it, and it can never be replaced. Our brain is our greatest resource!

Literary Link...

If you begin to understand what you are without trying to change it, then what you are undergoes a transformation.
—J. Krishnamurti

Gerald's Story

Gerald, a CEO for a large multi-state corporation, often challenged his department directors to view their jobs in a new way. Every job has parts of it that we enjoy, and every job has some less enjoyable aspects. "It's like cooking," he would explain, "occasionally you have to stop and do the dishes. Cooking is fun. Dishwashing isn't."

As we learn to live authentically, we can use Gerald's metaphor and do more cooking and spend less time dishwashing.

Reality Check

There is hope! If you identify your brain's innate preferences in four key areas and put into practice what you learn, the practical application of this knowledge on a daily basis can result in a more efficient use of your vital energy.

You may need to face uncomfortable realities. Are you in a career that doesn't even come close to matching your innate giftedness? Should you just up and quit?

Perhaps your sensory preference isn't being honored in your primary relationship. Should you just walk out?

Maybe you are not being appreciated for your

position on the gender continuum, or perhaps you are being shamed, if not punished, for your position on the EAI Continuum. Should you medicate your frustration and depression with alcohol, prescriptions, or some addictive process?

No, of course not. The issue of mismatches is real, however. It is to be hoped that you'll take the time to identify mismatches in your life and create a plan for resolving them.

Quick Fix

Let's review some strategies to help you plan a course of action—temporary fixes that you can implement, and tips that can assist you to get on with living a quality life as soon as possible. Here are several to consider.

First, begin to include activities in your life that honor your innate preferences. Or, if you've already started to do that, increase the number and frequency of those activities.

For example, if you have a job as an auditor and you realize this doesn't match your innate preferences and is draining your energy, develop hobbies or extracurricular activities that do match. Even if you aren't initially excited by the thought, make a point to pursue them anyway. Pay attention to how your brain and body feel as you engage in each activity, and move toward repeating those that help you to feel your best. The options are endless. Here are just a few examples:

- Join a local community board and get

involved with change

- Write poetry or short stories; join a creative writing club

- Travel; take trips to places you've only dreamed about

- Sign up for a watercolor class

- Attend jazz concerts; if you play the sax, join a jazz band

- Create some opportunities for spontaneity

- Read adventure, sci-fi, or personal growth books

If you are an elementary teacher and you discover that your giftedness relates more to systems orchestrated by the left posterior lobes, review these options:

- Develop family or school traditions and act on them

- Play on a team that has rules and follows them

- Develop routines that you can follow

- Solve crossword puzzles

- Volunteer in a library

- Get season tickets to sporting events

- Knit or crochet

- Plan a packaged cruise

- Read biographies or stories about team sports

If you are a psychiatrist or counselor and find that ten hours of one-to-one interaction is draining and that your brain bent is more aligned with left frontal lobe functions:

- Set specific financial goals and make decisions about investments

- Join a chess club, or some type of thinking competition

- Get involved with two-team sports, such as tennis or racquetball; or one-person activities like golf or jogging

- Try a home-improvement project

- Campaign for your favorite candidate during elections (if your brain leans toward extroversion)

- Chair a community board

- Read books about great leaders

- Study to increase the size of your vocabulary and join a debate club

If you are a department manager and discover that you are really more comfortable with activities that utilize functions from the right posterior lobes, try these on for size:

- Take a mini-vacation with your family and pets, or visit close friends

- Join a community choir or orchestra

- Find friends or associates to exercise with on a regular basis

- Join a social club

- Get involved in your community's drama group

- Read nonfiction nature books, biographies, or romances

- Learn how to speak a foreign language

- Hang out with a chef, interior decorator, or chaplain

Managing Stimulation

If your environment is too stimulating, take steps to carve out a niche for yourself where you can more effectively manage the amount of stimulation. Perhaps that is a room of your own or a private space somewhere in your home.

If your environment isn't offering you enough stimulation, up the ante. Try wearing a Walkman® whenever possible. Take breaks to connect with others or catch up on the news.

Make new friends who share your brain bent, and develop hobbies that match what your brain does easily—until it is financially responsible to make a career or life change (if possible).

Remember that a 100% match isn't doable and likely wouldn't be desirable anyway. A majority match is!

Literary Link...

> *Too many people overvalue what they are not, and undervalue what they are.*
> —Malcom Forbes

Janeen's Story

At one point during her teenage years, Janeen was grounded—briefly. You know the drill. It seemed like forever (and was probably unjustified)! To give her something to do, her English-teacher father suggested she memorize Edgar Guest's poem "Myself" and, much to his surprise (the father's, not Guest's) she did.

The first stanza began:

> I have to live with myself, and so
> I want to be fit for myself to know.
> I want to be able, as days go by,
> Always to look myself straight in the eye;
> I don't want to stand in the setting sun,
> And hate myself for things I've done.

Of course, at the time Janeen thought that last word, done, meant every teenager's favorite sins. Years went by and Janeen thought of the poem infrequently. One day, however, some of the words of that poem popped into her mind. And as both a student of, and a believer in, ongoing brain research, she began to perceive the poem in an entirely new light. She realized that it speaks to living authentically.

The words, "I want to be fit for myself to know," mean being who we were meant to be. That's just plain honest!

Wanting to always, "look myself straight in the eye" means honoring our brain's own unique giftedness. That's respect.

Not wanting to end life by hating oneself "for things I've done," now meant to Janeen, that in her twilight years, she wanted to avoid saying things like:

"I grew up wanting to be a teacher, but I never got the chance."

"I always wanted to dance, but I thought it was too late."

"I wish I would have entertained more, but my house was never clean enough."

"I would have loved to start my own business, but I didn't think I was smart enough."

"Why did I spend years as a ____ simply because that's what I was told to do in the first place?"

You get the idea. When we come to the end of our time on this planet, it may not be the things we did that may cause us regret as much as the things we didn't do—the choices we failed to make, the opportunities we were too fearful to seize, or the healthy risks we refused to take.

Fortunately, it's rarely too late to take positive steps toward owning who we are innately. Remember the poem, "When I am Old I Shall Wear Purple"? Now is the time to metaphorically wear purple, or whatever other color best suits our innate preferences. When we can do that with a family member or friend, so much the better!

Jon's Story
It was time for parent-teacher conferences. Sandwiched between his mother and father, Jon sat across the desk from his teacher. The boy looked at the floor as his father's words rushed out in bursts. "Miss Johnson, Jon is not getting A's in math and spelling. What are you going to do about it?"

Miss Johnson bit back both a smile and a retort. "What am I going to do about it", she thought to herself? "Give me a break!" Instead, she asked the father, rather off handedly, "How did you like math and spelling in school?"

There was a decided pause and then more words exploded into the air. "What do you think? I hated them both! Why do you think I'm insisting that Jon get A's? I don't want him to struggle in life like I've had to!" The father's already square jaw jutted out even further.

Miss Johnson sighed to herself. She'd experienced this scenario far too often. Why do so many parents place almost impossible expectations on their children? Especially when the parents had similar struggles!

Since there wasn't a definitive answer forthcoming, she began to talk with Jon's parents about the subjects in which the teenager appeared to be gifted—music, art, computers.

"Balderdash!" Jon's father said, "the computer market is flooded, and he can't make a living at music and art!"

Taking another tack, Miss Johnson asked, "What do you do for a living?"

"I'm an accountant," the man replied, "and a darned good one."

Taking another risk, the teacher asked, "And if you could do anything in the world you wanted to do, what would that be?"

The father's face became red, then turned pale, and ended up as a blotchy mix of the two. "And what difference would that be making?"

"Maybe no difference," the teacher replied, "but I am interested."

"I always wanted to be a chef," the father replied in an entirely different-sounding voice, while looking at the floor. Both Jon and his mother stared at the man in amazement. This was news to them. Big news!

Seizing the opportunity, Miss Johnson planted some seeds in the father's mind. Seeds about helping Jon find his own giftedness. Seeds about the difference between doing one's best versus feeling pressured to get A's in every subject. Seeds about Jon and his father enrolling at the junior college for some evening classes on cooking and art. The best part was that Jon's father seemed actually open to the idea!

Miss Johnson smiled to herself and thought, "It's definitely worth the effort! They both may be on their way to find their own paths."

Iyanla Vanzant addressed this in *Acts of Faith*: "Many of us have said, "I am tired of struggling!" Well, guess what?... When you stop struggling, things get better. Struggle goes against the flow. It creates exhaustion in the mind and body. When you are exhausted you get sick. If you are sick, you must make a decision and commitment to do everything in your power to get better. The power is in the commitment never to do what makes you sick. The key is the decision never to tire of doing what is best, good, and right for you."

Live by Design
As statesman Oliver Wendell Holmes said, "The human mind, once exposed to a new idea, never returns to its original dimensions."

Your mind wants to grow and be stretched, to be discovered and energized. Even more importantly, it wants to be respected and honored. It wants you to collaborate with it, not by default but by design!

It's time for you to make a difference. Go now. Write your own stories. Debunk the myths and invent new truths. Live your own innate preferences and create your own miracles.

Pablo Casals said, "And what do we teach our children in school? We teach them that two and two make four, and that Paris is the capital of France. When will we also teach them what they are? We should say to each of them: 'Do you know what you are? You are a marvel. You are unique. In all the world there is no child exactly like you...' You may become a Shakespeare, a Michelangelo, a Beethoven. You have the capacity for anything. Yes, you are a marvel.'"

Those very same words could have been written about you, as an adult. Yes, you are a marvel. Let your gifts shine through because there will never be another you. The new applications and personal experiences—in narrative or poetry or picture or dance—are for you to create. You can't go back and make a brand new start, but you can start from now and make a brand new ending.

Empowered with this new information, your journey's just begun. As the song says, "we've only just begun"—to live...

Einstein said, "Nothing happens until something moves." It's time to get moving. Get moving at the speed of life. Yours! The life you save could be your own.

> *Happiness is a journey,*
> *not a destination.*
> *So work like you don't need money.*
> *Love like you've never been hurt.*
> *And dance like no one is watching!*
> —Anonymous

SELECTED
BIBLIOGRAPHY

Albom, Mitch. *Tuesdays with Morrie*. NY: Doubleday, 1997.

Baker, Mary Anne, ed. *Sex Differences in Human Performance*. NY: John Wiley & Sons, 1987.

Bandler, Richard. *Using Your Brain for a Change*. UT: Real People, 1985.

Bandler, Richard, and John Grinder. *Frogs into Princes*. UT: Real People, 1979.

Bartlett, John. *Familiar Quotations, 10th edition*. NY: Bartleby, 2000.

Benson, Herbert, M.D., with William Proctor. *Your Maximum Mind*. NY: Avon Books, 1987.

Benziger, I. Katherine. *Thriving in Mind: The Art and Science of Using Your Whole Brain*. TX: KBA Publishing, 2000.

Bost, Brent W., MD. *The Hurried Woman Syndrome*. NY: Vantage Press, 2001.

Brothers, Joyce. *What Every Woman Should Know about Men*. NY: Ballantine Books, 1981.

Brynie, Faith Hickman. *101 Questions Your Brain Has Asked about Itself but Couldn't Answer until Now.* Brookfield, Connecticut: The Millbrook Press, 1998.

Buzan, Tony. *Make The Most of Your Mind.* NY: Linden Press, 1977.

_____. *Use Both Sides of Your Brain.* NY: E.P. Dutton, 1983.

Caine, Geoffrey, Renate N. Caine, Sam Crowell. *MindShifts.* AZ: Zephyr Press, 1999.

Carter, Rita, ed. *Exploring Consciousness.* Berkeley: University of California Press, 2002.

_____. *Mapping the Mind.* Berkeley: University of California Press, 1998.

Charles A. Dana Foundation. *Gray Matters. Men, Women and the Brain.* NY: Dana Alliance for Brain Initiatives, 2000

Columbia Encyclopedia, The, 6th ed. New York: Columbia University Press, 2002.

Conway, Jim. *Men in Mid-Life Crisis.* Illinois: David C. Cook Publishing Company, 1978.

Cruise, Robert J., and Peter Blitchington. *Temperament Inventory.* Berrien Springs, MI: Andrews University Press, 1977.

_____. *Understanding Your Temperament.* Berrien Springs, MI: Andrews University Press, 1979.

Damasio, Antonio. *Descartes' Error.* NY: Avon Books, 1994.

Diamond, Marian, and Janet Hopson. *Magic Trees of the Mind*. NY: Dutton,1998.

Dole, Nathan Haskell, ed. *Familiar Quotations, 10th ed.* NY: Bartleby, 2000.

Emerson, Ralph Waldo. *Self Reliance and Other Essays.* NY: Dover Publishers, 1993

Gardner, Howard. *The Shattered Mind.* NY: Vintage Books, 1976.

Giuffre, Kenneth. *The Care and Feeding of Your Brain.* Franklin Lakes, NJ: Career Press, 1999.

Gopnik, Allison, Andrew N. Meltzoff, and Patricia K. Kuhl. *The Scientist in The Crib.* NY: Morrow, 1999.

Gray, John. *Men, Women and Relationships: Making Peace with the Opposite Sex.* Oregon: Beyond Words Publishing, 1993.

Greenfield, Susan, con. ed. *Brain Power: Working out the Human Mind.* Britain: Element Books Limited, 1999.

Guest, Edgar A. *Collected Verse.* NY: Buccaneer Books, 1996

Gurian, Michael, and Patricia Henley, with Terry Trueman. *Boys and Girls Learn Differently!* San Francisco: Jossey-Bass, a Wiley Company, 2001.

Hafen, Brent Q., et. al. *Mind/Body Health.* Massachusetts: Allyn and Bacon, 1996.

Hamer, Dean, and Peter Copeland. *Our Genes: Why They Matter More than You Think.* NY: Doubleday, 1998.

Healy, Jane M. *Endangered Minds: Why Children Don't Think and What We Can Do about It*. NY: Simon & Schuster, 1990.

Healy, Jane M. *Failure To Connect: How Computers Affect Our Children's Minds—for Better and Worse*. NY: Simon & Schuster, 1998.

Herrmann, Ned. *The Whole Brain Business Book*. NY: McGraw-Hill, 1996.

_____. *The Creative Brain*. North Carolina: The Ned Herrmann Group, 1993.

Hinton, S. E. *The Outsiders*. NY: Viking Press, 1967.

Howard, Pierce J. *The Owner's Manual for the Brain: Everyday Applications from Mind-Brain Research*. TX: Bard Press, 2000.

International Bible Society. *Holy Bible: New International Version*. Grand Rapids, MI: The Zondervan Publishing House, 1973, 1978, 1984.

Isherwood, Christopher. *The Berlin Stories: The Last of Mr. Norris and Goodbye to Berlin*. NY: New Directions Publishing, 1988.

Jensen, Eric. *Teaching With the Brain In Mind*. Alexandria, VA: ASCD, 1998.

Joy, Donald M., PhD. *Bonding*. Nashville, TN: Word Books, 1985.

Jung, C.G. *Psychological Types*. NJ: Princeton University Press, 1971).

Keirsey, David W., and Marilyn Bates. *Please Understand Me*. Del Mar, CA: Prometheus Nemesis Book Co., 1978, 1984. Leornian Press, 2000.

Kidd, Parris M., Jack Challem, and Victoria Dolby Toews. *Phosphatidylserine.* NY: McGraw-Hill/Contemporary Books, 1998).

Kidd, Parris, and Stephen A. Levine. *Antioxidant Adaptation: Its Role in Free Radical Pathology.* California: Allergy Research Group, 1986.

Kotulak, Ronald. *Inside The Brain.* KS: Andrews McMeal Publishing, 1997.

LeDoux, Joseph. *The Emotional Brain.* NY: Touchstone, 1996.

Levine, Mel, M.D. *A Mind at A Time.* NY: Simon & Schuster, 2002.

Lewis, Thomas, M.D.; Amini, Fari Amini; M.D., and Richard Lannon, M.D. *A General Theory of Love.* NY: Vintage Books, 2001.

Luria, A.R. *The Mind of a Mnemonist.* Cambridge, MA: Harvard University Press, 1968.

_____. *The Working Brain.* NY: Penguine Books Ltd., 1973.

Luddington-Hoe, Susan, with Susan K. Golant. *How to Have a Smarter Baby.* NY: Bantam Books, 1985

McCarthy, Bernice. *About Learning.* Wauconda, IL: About Learning, Inc., 1996.

_____. *About Teaching.* Wauconda, IL: About Learning, Inc., 2000.

_____. *4MAT Workshop Syllabus.* Wauconda, IL: About Learning, Inc., 2000.

McGraw, Phillip C, PhD. *Self Matters: Creating Your Life From Inside Out*. NY: Simon & Schuster Source, 2001.

McWilliams, Peter. *You Can't Afford the Luxury of a Single Negative Thought*. CA: Prelude Press, 1995.

Miller, Lawrence, PhD. *Inner Natures: Brain, Self & Personality*. NY: Ballantine Books, 1990.

Moir, Anne & Jessel, David. *Brain Sex: the Real Difference Between Men & Women*. NY: Carol Publishing Group, 1991.

Nicholson, John. *Men & Women: How Different are They?* Oxford: Oxford University Press, 1984.

Ornstein, Robert, M.D., *Multimind: A New Way of Looking at Human Behavior*. NY: Doubleday, 1986.

_____. *The Right Mind: Making Sense of the Hemispheres*. NY: Harcourt Brace & Company, 1997.

_____. *The Roots of the Self: Unraveling the Mystery of Who We Are*. San Francisco, HarperCollins, 1995.

Ornstein, Robert, M.D., and Charles Swencionis. *The Healing Brain: A Scientific Reader*. NY: The Guilford Press, 1990.

Ornstein, Robert, M.D., and Richard F. Thompson. *The Amazing Brain*. MA: Houghton Mifflin Company, 1984.

Ornstein, Robert, M.D., and David Sobel. *The Healing Brain: Breakthrough Discoveries about How the Brain Keeps Us Healthy*. NY: Simon & Schuster, 1999. Cambridge, MA: Malor Books, 1987, 1999.

Pearce, Joseph Chilton. *Evolution's End: Claiming the Potential of Our Intelligence*. San Francisco: Harper, 1992.

_____. *The Roots of Intelligence* (Audiocassette). Colorado: Sounds True Audio Tapes, 1991.

Pert, Candace B. *Molecules of Emotions*. NY: Scribner, 1997.

_____. *Your Body is Your Subconscious Mind* (Audiocassettes). Colorado: Sounds True Audio Tapes, 2000.

Preamble to the Constitution of the World Health Organization as adopted by the International Health Conference, NY, 19-22 June, 1946; signed on 22 July 1946 by the representatives of 61 States (Official Records of the World Health Organization, no. 2, p. 100) and entered into force on 7 April 1948.

Quartz, Steven R., and Terrence J. Sejnowski. *Liars, Lovers, and Heroes: What the New Brain Science Reveals about How We Become Who We Are*. NY: HarperCollins Publishers Inc., 2002.

Ramachandran, V.S. *Phantoms in the Brain*. NY: Morrow, 1998.

Restak, Richard, MD. *Mozart's Brain and the Fighter Pilot*. NY: Harmony Books, 2001.

_____. *Mysteries of the Mind*. Washington, DC: National Geographic, 2000.

_____. *The Brain: The Last Frontier*. NY: Warner Books, Inc., 1980.

_____. *The Brain*. NY: Bantam Books, 1984.

_____. *The Brain has a Mind of its Own*. NY: Harmony Books, 1991.

_____. *The Secret Life of the Brain*. NY: Dana Press and Joseph Henry Press, 2001.

Ratey, John J. *A User's Guide to the Brain: Perception, Attention, and the Four Theaters of the Brain*. NY: Vintage Books, 2002.

Roizen, Michael R., MD. *Real Age, Are You as Young as You Can Be?* NY: Cliff Street Books, an imprint of HarperCollins Publishers, 2000.

Selye, Hans. *The Stress of Life*. NY: McGraw-Hill, 1956.

Siegel, Daniel J. *The Developing Mind*. NY: The Guilford Press, 1999.

Silverstein, Shel. *Where the Sidewalk Ends: Poems and Drawings*. NY: HarperCollins Juvenile Books, 1974.

Simpson, James B. *Simpson's Contemporary Quotations, Revised Edition*. NY: HarperCollins Publishers, 1997.

Sommer, Elyse, with Dorris Weiss. *Metaphors Dictionary*. Detroit, Michigan: Visible Ink Press, 1996.

Sousa, David A. *How the Brain Learns: A Classroom Teacher's Guide*. Alexandria, VA: ASCD, 1995.

_____. *Learning Manual For How The Brain Learns*. Thousand Oaks, CA: Corwin Press, Inc., 1998.

_____. *How the Special Needs Brain Learns*. Thousand Oaks, CA: Corwin Press, Inc., 2001.

_____. *How the Brain Learns: A Classroom Teacher's Guide*. Alexandria, VA: ASCD, 1995.

Sprenger, Marilee. *Learning & Memory: The Brain in Action*. Alexandria, VA: ASCD, 1999.

Steinem, Gloria. *Revolution from Within*. Boston: Little, Brown and Company, 1992.

Stine, Jean Marie. *Super Brain Power*. NJ: Prentis Hall, 2000.

Stump, Jane Barr, PhD. *What's the Difference?* NY: William Morrow & Company, Inc., 1985.

Sylwester, Robert. *A Celebration of Neurons: An Educator's Guide To The Human Brain*. Alexandria, VA: ASCD, 1995.

_____. *A Biological Brain in a Cultural Classroom*. Thousand Oaks, CA: Corwin Press, Inc., 2000.

Tanenbaum, Joe. *Male & Female Realities, Understanding the Opposite Sex*. Nevada: Robert Erdmann Publishing, 1990.

Trelease, Jim. *The Read-Aloud Handbook*. NY: Penguin Books, 5th ed., 2001.

United States in Literature, The (textbook anthology). IL: Scott Foresman, 1991.

Vanzant, Iyanla. *Acts of Faith*. KS: Fireside Press, 1993.

Wade, Nicholas, ed. *The Science Times Book of the Brain*. NY: NY Times, 1998.

Williamson, Marianne, *A Return to Love: Reflections on the Principles of a Course in Miracles*. NY: HarperCollins Publishers, 1996.

Wilson, Glenn. *The Great Sex Divide: A study of Male-Female Differences*. London: Peter Owen, 1989.

Wonder, Jacquelyn, and Priscilla Donovan. *Whole Brain Thinking*. NY: Ballantine Books, 1984.

ABOUT THE
AUTHORS